THE ENCHANTED WORLD
OF
JESSIE M. KING

Jessie M. King, greetings card, 'My Thoughts like Winged Birds', c1909. 27.3 cm × 22.9 cm.
Barclay Lennie collection.

THE ENCHANTED WORLD OF JESSIE·M·KING

BY COLIN WHITE

CANONGATE

TO THE MEMORY OF
Merle Taylor
1909–85

First published in 1989 in Great Britain
by Canongate Publishing Ltd
17 Jeffrey Street, Edinburgh EH1 1DR

The publishers acknowledge subsidy from the Scottish Arts Council towards the
publication of this volume.

Typeset by C. R. Barber & Partners, Fort William, Scotland.
Printed and bound in Great Britain by Eagle Press, Blantyre, Scotland.

British Library Cataloguing in Publication Data
White, Colin
The Enchanted World of Jessie M. King.
1. Scottish visual arts. King, Jessie M.
I. Title
709'.2'4
ISBN 0-86241-235-8

Contents

Jessie M. King, 'Richard Yea and Nay', 1912. Pen, ink, watercolour and silver. 33 cm × 45.1 cm.
Private collection.

List of Illustrations

Unless otherwise stated all works listed below are by Jessie M. King. The chapter head and tail pieces are decorative illustrations from *The High History of the Holy Graal*, *The Defence of Guenevere* and *A House of Pomegranates* (1)

Introduction

Jessie Marion King was the most important Scottish illustrator of the twentieth century. She studied at the Glasgow School of Art under the great Fra Newbery and numbered among her contemporaries Charles Rennie Mackintosh, the Macdonald sisters and those other artists who, together, established what has come to be known as the Glasgow Style.

In adult life she was looked upon as 'kenspeckle', an old word meaning 'conspicuous', that was still used by the people of south-west Scotland where she eventually settled. She was credited by some with second sight, and there were even those who believed that her gifts were 'supernatural'. Her habits did little to discourage this conviction. She dressed like a witch in a flowing black cloak, buckled shoes and a wide-brimmed black hat looking, as she herself acknowledged, like an advertisement for Sandeman's Port. Titbits of her individualistic behaviour were relished: how she darned black stockings with patches of brightly coloured wool, or how she could be seen every week on her hands and knees outside her house drawing patterns on the cobbles with little wedges of scouring-stone. Visitors to Kirkcudbright, where she lived, were always told of 'Poland', the nickname given to her studio, where the floor was strewn with the old chamber pots she used as containers for her colours.

The legend fitted in with the common preconception of the artist as the 'outsider', the social oddity, and ignored the fact that a questioning of the fashions and mores of society was one of the outward urges of an artist's creativity. Jessie M. King adopted her large Breton hat to protect her fair complexion from the sun. She chose her mannish shoes because they were practical and comfortable. The coloured darning wool was to add a touch of gaiety to otherwise sober black stockings, and her long skirts were worn as much to hide her heavy body and thick ankles as to complete her costume. Jessie M. King was much more than the sum of her whimsies, and any assessment of her art must look beyond these superficial features of her personality.

It was in order to secure the most important source of first-hand information about the artist that what had initially been the gathering of occasional material became purposeful research. Merle Taylor, the artist's only child, was in her seventies and in failing health when this book was planned. She graciously allowed me access to family papers and photographs, and spent many hours patiently coping with questions which must often have seemed naïve and, at times, impossible to answer. Those who speak of Jessie

M. King's later 'pot-boiling years' would say that her greatest work was done before Merle had reached an age of discernment. Nevertheless, Merle Taylor was able to offer a unique insight into her mother's work as well as her life. Without her help this book would not have been written, and it is a cause of sadness that she did not live to see it through to completion.

In mentioning some of the people who have generously helped with my researches I hope I shall not be offending the many others to whom I am also indebted. I would particularly like to thank Anne and Peyton Skipwith and, through them, the Fine Art Society Ltd for their advice and their kindness in lending me both printed and photographic material; Michael Heseltine, Catherine Porter and Elizabeth Tate of Sotheby's, and the departments of paintings at both Christie's and Phillips for supplying photographs; Robin de Beaumont for his generosity in allowing me access to his work notes; Lionel Lambourne and Linda Parry of the Victoria and Albert Museum, Christine Woods of the Whitworth Art Gallery, Manchester, and Miss B. Gregory of the Courtauld Institute for their help with Jessie M. King's fabrics and crafted items; and David Brass, Nial Devitt, Andrena Dobbin, Olaf Eue, Mike Finnie, Dr J. L. Gordon, Robin Greer, Professor Thomas Howarth, Gerald and Celia Larner, Barclay Lennie, Cordelia Oliver, Louise Ross, Martin Steenson and James Young—all devotees of Jessie M. King's art—for bringing to my notice unusual items. I must thank Alan Marks in Berlin and Graham Dry in Munich for their great help with Jessie M. King's German work. I would also like to thank Mme Passuth of the Musée d'Art Moderne in Paris for allowing me to root through boxes of papers in the archives and emerge dirty but triumphant with the correspondence relating to Jessie M. King's nursery exhibition of 1913. In Scotland I would like to thank Jocelyn Grigg and Ian Monie of the Glasgow School of Art for their help in tracing Jessie M. King's path through the school; Martin Hopkinson and his colleagues of the Hunterian Museum; Rosemary Watt of the Glasgow Museum and Stanley Simpson and his colleagues of the National Library of Scotland, who allowed me to work through their holdings of Jessie M. King material and supplied me with study photographs. I would also, very shamefacedly, like to thank Niall Duncan of Castle Douglas for allowing me to photograph the Jessie M. King pottery he owns, and for being so calm and understanding when I broke one of his treasures.

Finally, I would like to thank the many friends my wife and I made in both Kirkcudbright and Arran—people who were kind enough to invite us into their homes to talk about the artist. Tom Collin, Curator of the Stewartry Museum in Kirkcudbright, actually opened up the museum one night to allow me to photograph one of the exhibits. If I may be allowed to single out one person to represent these generous individuals I would pick Jessie Cumming, the 'Brownie' of this book. She attended Merle Taylor's every need in her last years and acted as my link with Kirkcudbright when I was unable to go there in person. To all who have helped I offer my grateful thanks and hope that this book goes some way to meeting their expectations.

Colin White
September 1988

CHAPTER ONE

The Manse

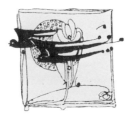

Jessie M. King was an illustrator of dreams. She created a world in which a dimly remembered Celtic past allowed fantasy and reality to blend together and bring both delight and confusion to the mind. She drew slender, unsubstantial knights and princesses, fairies and nymphs. She dressed them in gowns of the finest lawn and armour of burnished silver in fashions borrowed from the same Renaissance and Oriental styles that had inspired the pre-Raphaelites and their followers. Consequently, her characters belonged to no time and no place outside the eternities of dreams. Her art spoke of stillness and privacy. Her life, by contrast, was public and active. To the outside world she was bold and expansive, a leader and organiser. No matter what pools of silence and reserve lay within, her persona was one of laughing good nature and exuberant friendliness.

In her more fanciful moments Jessie King claimed descent from a Major Weir who was burned at the stake as a warlock in the time of Mary Queen of Scots. More immediately, she was the daughter of the Revd James Waters King, minister of the church of New Kilpatrick at Bearsden, near Glasgow. He was born on 15 August 1836, the eldest son of William Clark King, a miller of Fintry, in the hills to the north of Glasgow. The mid-Victorian society he grew up in was patriarchal, God-fearing and conservative. Self-improvement and the attainment of self-sufficiency were respectable aims for a young man. Education was a means to this end and there was no more praiseworthy ambition than to serve the Almighty, one's country and one's fellow men. James King received the message and decided to enter the church.

He took his bachelor's degree at the University of Glasgow in 1857 and his MA three years later. While still a divinity student he worked as a missionary for the Church of Scotland in Trom, a parish of some 5000 people in one of the poorest districts of Glasgow. His duties were to call from door to door, distributing tracts and offering spiritual advice. On his recommendation the Elders of the Church of Scotland built for the community a church which, from its address in Havannah Street, eventually became known as the Plantation Church. At its consecration in 1860 James King, although still a licentiate and not yet ordained, was appointed to take charge of its running. Two years later he was made full minister. He organised educational facilities and savings schemes, and maintained contact with his parishioners, despite the size of the organisation he had built up, by doing a daily round of fieldwork with his helpers.

In 1865 he was moved to the church of Killearn, near Glasgow, where his

2 *The Reverend James King, circa 1895.*

3 *Bearsden, circa 1890, from a contemporary photograph.*

4 *The Manse, Bearsden, circa 1890.*

abilities as an efficient and caring minister came to the notice of the Duke of Montrose. In 1870, in the last act of private patronage to take place within the church before a new ruling allowed congregations to elect their own clergy, the Duke appointed James King to the large diocese of New Kilpatrick, as it was then called. When the railways came the parish kept its name but the town became Bearsden to avoid confusion with the adjacent Old Kilpatrick. Bearsden, then some twenty minutes away from Glasgow by train, was a community of 5000, mainly middle-class people, and was developing into a fashionable residential area for business commuters. The outer fringes of the parish led to more open country where there were farms with dairy cattle, oats and barley, and a few small coal mining areas. At first the Revd King was able to do his round on horseback but, as the population grew and his work increased, he acquired a pony and phaeton and, eventually, a coachman who also did duty as the Manse gardener.

The Manse itself was a three-storey house of limewashed brick built in 1835 on the crest of a mound facing the church. A contemporary account described it as 'a neat little edifice in the English cottage style'. There were five bedrooms for the family and two attics for the servants. At the front a lawn sloped down to a shrubbery and a copse of old beech trees. Beyond these, in the dip, were the two large stone buildings of the stables and the coach-house. From here a narrow road wound round the wall that protected the south part of the churchyard where the oldest gravestones stood. When the sun was low and the shadows long it was still possible to make out the worn seventeenth-century inscriptions carved in the old Scottish lettering that the Glasgow Stylists were later to rediscover. Behind the house was an orchard and a sheltered garden overlooking the glebe in which the cow, the pigs and, eventually, Jessie's rabbits were kept. At the bottom of the glebe was a burn and, beyond this, the land rose up again as the copse of beeches which was to appear as the home of wood-sprites in many of Jessie's drawings.

On 6 April 1869, shortly before he was granted the living of New Kilpatrick, James King married Mary Ann Anderson, a Lanark girl some thirteen years younger than himself, the daughter of a local banker. Their marriage produced four daughters in succession followed, in 1876, by a son, James Graham. The first child, born in 1871, was named Evangeline Ann Steele, after her maternal grandmother. As the oldest daughter, Eva, as she was called, became her mother's right arm in the running of the house and the management of the younger children. She grew up capable and dependable, and had the duties and mantle of a future housewife thrust on her at an early age. She took care of her father after her mother's death and married in 1902 only after her father died. She gave birth to a large family in a relatively short time, a fact which occasioned a remark from Jessie some years later when she was admonishing her own daughter Merle. 'Only those people,' she said, 'who are the aunts of two sets of twins and a single child can put their elbows on the table at mealtimes.'

The Kings' second daughter, Adah Mary Waters, was born in February 1872. She was the rebel of the family. Independently minded, wilful and difficult in her parents' eyes she was, to the outside world, bright, individualistic, noncomformist and an altogether exciting person. While still in her teens she was permitted to use a legacy from a benevolent aunt and leave home more, one suspects, to relieve the pressures within the household than to allow her to exploit the natural resources of vigorous youth. As she was good at languages, after school she used her legacy to travel to France, Germany, Italy and Asia Minor. She eventually settled in Berlin and set up as an English teacher. Her French was as fluent as her German and, after the First World War, she went to live in Paris and teach there. Even as a child Adah was the fashion-conscious member of the family. To her the trees in the Manse garden did not mean a good climb as they did to Jessie, but a scenic backdrop for graceful poses. The other girls wore tams and bonnets. Adah wore hats.

The third child, Margaret Dun, or Peggy as she was called from the start, was born in September 1873. She had some of Adah's vivacity but channelled her energies in a more conventional manner. She was the first of the daughters to be allowed a career, and later trained as a schoolteacher at Queen Margaret College in Glasgow. In 1900, at the age of twenty-seven, she died in childbirth, along with her baby, while staying with Adah in Berlin.

The Kings' youngest daughter, Jessie Marion, was born on 20 March 1875, exactly a year before their son Graham. Jessie, like Peggy, was an Anderson in appearance. She had her mother's broad nose and slightly prognathous jaw which caused her lower lip to curve in an attractive scroll and merge with her beautifully shaped chin. Her eyes were wide-set and of a penetrating blue. Their colour was enhanced by ringlets of long golden hair which, when she was older, she often wore coiled about her head. Her fair complexion, like Merle's after her, was sensitive to sunlight, and a caricature sketch of her, done one summer in France many years later, showed her veiled to the eyes like a Tuareg, for protection.

As her sisters grew taller and more slender, Jessie seemed to retain the chunkiness of her babyhood. Family tradition had it that, in accordance with

5 *Jessie M. King aged three, 1878.*

the law of hand-me-downs, Eva had the new clothes; Adah was forever complaining at having to wear her sister's cast-offs; Peggy, ever adaptable, accepted her role as third in line; while Jessie had to have her clothes newly designed because it took two dresses to make one for her. A photograph taken in 1885 of all five children dressed for a wedding gives clues to their characters. The girls are wearing slippers rather than their everyday boots, and their hair is severely combed back to accommodate the coronets of flowers on their little veils. Eva, taller than the others, is obviously the leader. Adah, looking beautiful, with an expression of complete innocence, has evidently worked on her ballerina's pose down to the deliberate placing of her feet. Peggy, with her large eyes, shows something of the uncertainty that lay beneath the surface calm of her nature during her short life. Graham, for all his nine years, looks wise and nonchalant, his hair beautifully parted, and wearing a flower in the buttonhole of his Norfolk jacket. Jessie looks solidly determined, with an air of angry defiance about the fact that she is having trouble with her drawers.

6

The King Children photographed in 1885, from the left: Graham, Eva, Adah, Peggy and Jessie.

7
Mary MacNab (pictured right) with Jessie M. King (centre, in shadow) and Merle Taylor, circa 1918.

When Jessie was born, Mary King, with three other children under the age of five, needed help in the home, and so Mary McNab, a young girl from Strachur at the head of Loch Fyne in the Highlands, was engaged as a nursemaid. Maime, as she was called to avoid confusion with Mrs King, was tiny and sardonic. She was a strict Presbyterian and an ardent churchgoer, with Gaelic as her first language. She already had experience of looking after her younger brothers and sisters at home and, at fifteen, was capable, pert and efficient. From the beginning she looked upon Jessie as her property and responsibility. When Jessie got a home of her own Maime came to join her. When Jessie's daughter was born Maime became her nurse as she had been Jessie's. Everybody knew Maime. People respected her and were a little frightened of her. Friends of Jessie's always included greetings and good wishes to Maime when they wrote. A fellow artist of Jessie's once described Maime, as 'the faithful Miss McNab who, I always feel, gives a certain stolidity to an otherwise very romantic household'.

The girls did not want for anything at home but neither were they pampered. The only holiday they had as children was one isolated week of wonder when their father was able to exchange pulpits with a colleague at Lamlash on Arran, and Jessie was able to see, for the first time, the magic of the island that was to become a second home to her. They were allowed pets and toys in moderation. Jessie's first love was Jane, her Dutch doll. Even though her hair was painted on and her nose a mere triangular wedge of wood, Jane was far superior to Eva's pallid wax-faced French doll because she was jointed. With a little manipulation she could assume any attitude, pugilistic or affectionate. She could stride across the room and, with assistance, could kneel alongside the other children at prayers. The girls had Scottie dogs and a huge hutch of rabbits which stood by the orchard near the pigs and the cow. As a child Jessie always had difficulty in reconciling her love for God with His evident preference for animal sacrifice over Abel's offering of fruits. The rabbits became her responsibility and, at the age of ten, she made a new hutch for them because, as she put it, she was worried by their 'arithmetical qualities'. She was always good with her hands, and she sawed and dovetailed the wood and countersank the screws herself. Her greatest moment of pride came when the gardener admired her finished work and declared, 'Aye, ye should ha' been a laddie'.

Discipline at the Manse was strict. Meals were regular and orderly, and religious attendance and punctiliousness were compulsory. Sabbath observance, or at least its awareness, remained with the sisters throughout their lives. Adah, in a travel diary of 1924, described one Sunday in Rome when she attended service at the English church three times. On another occasion, somebody who knew Jessie's Sabbath commitments, felt the need to comment, at the bottom of one of her sketches, that she had drawn on a Sunday, 'little devil that she is'.

Jessie, like her sisters, was sent to the local Dame's School run by a Miss Smillie in her own house. Every morning, children of various ages and abilities, from all social backgrounds, assembled in Miss Smillie's dining room and sat round her with their slates and slate pencils, chalk and cleaning rag, to be instructed in the fundamentals of reading, writing, a little arithmetic and a great deal of religious instruction. At the age of five or six Jessie graduated to the local Parish School, the 'Old School', which was maintained by the church and was used after hours for lectures, dancing classes and the Parish library. Jessie was intelligent and alert. She had a good memory for poetry but lacked the capacity for sustained thought or concentrated attack on any subject other than her great joy, drawing. Her teachers saw her natural talent and encouraged her to think of going to the Glasgow School of Art to become a 'real artist'.

Her first soundings of her parents about what, to her, was a perfectly feasible idea, were either ignored or placated with deprecatory noises. When the pleas became more urgent, Jessie's parents ruled the idea as out of the question. There was no doubt in their minds that Jessie was talented but, to them, a career in art meant a bohemian life, and this was no calling for the daughter of a minister of the Church of Scotland. In those days the youngest daughter of a middle-class family did not go out to work to earn money. To do so was a slight on the ability of the father to support his family. The first aim of a girl was to make a good marriage. Teaching was permissible, for one could rationalise that this involved public service. Nursing, as a profession, was in its infancy, and social welfare work was a voluntary pastime that ministers' families and ladies of leisure practised. Painting and drawing came under the heading of accomplishments. One learned to do these as hobbies, just as one learned the piano or needlework. To want to take this up as a profession was frivolous and irresponsible. To Jessie, though, art was her way of expressing herself, just as others might use language or song. It was an extension of herself in pictorial terms: an acknowledgement of the world around her in drawing. The more she persisted in her determination with tears, temper and threats of leaving home, the more obdurate her parents became. Mary King was in no way disposed to be as lenient with Jessie as she had been with Adah and so, when Jessie came home from school, she had to suppress her enthusiasm and, to avoid trouble, hide her work in the bushes at the bottom of the garden until it was safe for her to bring it into the house. Only Maime understood but, like Mrs King, she saw Glasgow as a hostile environment with its crowds, drunkenness, dirt and disease. For Jessie, though, a move from Bearsden to Glasgow was a move outwards and upwards. There were splendid shops and arcades. There were cafés and tea rooms better, it was said, than those in London. There were theatres and picture galleries, gas lighting and the new horse-drawn trams. And, above all, there was the art school in Rose Street.

In the end it was the Revd King who capitulated. A compromise was reached. Jessie would be allowed to leave school before her matriculation and apply for the diploma course at the art school with a view to becoming an art teacher. She submitted a portfolio of her work and was offered a place. In September 1891, at the age of sixteen, Jessie enrolled at Queen Margaret College, in her father's name because she was still a minor, to start a foundation course in anatomy. Peggy was already there as a matriculated student training to be a teacher, and her chaperoning of Jessie was one of the conditions of her parents' consent. One year later, in September 1892, Jessie achieved her ambition and registered as a full-time day student at the Glasgow School of Art under its celebrated principal Fra Newbery.

8
The King family photographed outside the Manse, 1891.

CHAPTER TWO

Fra Newbery

9
Fra Newbery, circa 1890.

Francis Henry Newbery, the headmaster of the Glasgow School of Art, preferred to be called Fra Newbery for fear that the 'F' in his initials might be misinterpreted as 'Fred'. The resulting ecclesiastical overtones both satisfied his purpose and added to the dignity of his authority. He was born in Membury, Devon in 1854 and studied painting, first at Bridport School of Art, and then at the South Kensington Schools where, on graduating, he joined the staff. He was appointed director of the Glasgow School of Art in 1885 at the age of thirty-one, inheriting a small provincial art school, 'The Glasgow Institute', which occupied a portion of the Corporation Galleries at the junction of Sauchiehall Street and Rose Street. Under previous headmasters the teaching had been traditional and formal, discipline loose and attendance lax. Although Newbery's predecessor, Thomas Symmonds, had done much to raise the standards of the school, his annual report of 1884, the year before Newbery's arrival, deplored the fact that many of the students attended sporadically, 'doing very little good to themselves and reflecting no credit on those who are responsible for their progress'. The number of medals awarded to the school's most talented pupils at the annual National Competition at South Kensington had increased during Symmonds' reign of office but the number of works actually accepted for consideration were still miserably few. Out of 5807 works by the Glasgow students that had been submitted in 1883 only sixty-two had been selected for competition.

The curriculum of the Glasgow School of Art when Newbery arrived was devoted almost entirely to aspects of picture making. Decorative art was confined to one course in decorative plaster-work and one in stained glass. Fra Newbery, although primarily a painter himself, felt strongly that an education in applied art was as essential to a complete artist as one in fine art. He believed that an artist-craftsman was far better equipped for a successful career and that this type of education could only lead to an improvement in the quality of design and, hence, the beauty of the environment.

It took Fra Newbery three years to persuade the Board of Governors to allow him to establish a decorative arts department with adequate teaching and workshop facilities. His task was a difficult one. The School, like all those in the country, was state-aided and was subject to rules laid down by the Board of Education in London. Public benefactors were few and their support was limited. An industrialist who wished to be known as a patron of learning was able to secure a better advertisement for himself by an endowment to a university where training for some 'useful' occupation might result from his beneficence. Fra Newbery's requests for extra staff and facilities were received with bewilderment and hostility. He argued that art could make a valuable contribution to the community. The graduates of the school could benefit industry if they were given the right training, and manufacturers of furniture, carpets and wallpaper in Glasgow could work with them, to their mutual advantage.

Eventually, Newbery convinced the captains of industry on the Board of Governors, and artist-craftsmen were appointed to the staff to teach pottery, bookbinding, wood-carving and glass staining, together with, as the prospectus worded it, 'artistic needlework taught by a lady'. Newbery turned his small art school into a family with himself as head of the household. Staff and faculty mixed together, both in the studio and in the dining room, but familiarity was discouraged. To his face he was always 'Mr Newbery'. Behind his back he was always 'The Fra'.

From the start, Newbery encouraged each new student to take a complete course through to diploma standard, for he looked upon the diploma as a passport to a job if the student's hopes of becoming a 'real artist' were disappointed. He was flexible in his teaching methods and was prepared to adjust a syllabus to suit a particular student's needs but, within these parameters, he maintained a strict discipline and his pupils had to work hard if they wanted to continue their courses. He approved of equal opportunities for women in art, both in their training and in the openings that might be offered them afterwards. He welcomed them in his school but was still a prisoner of many of the prejudices of his time. He would have supported, for instance, a comment on Jessie M. King's drawing 'Pelleas and Melisande' in *The Studio* magazine in 1901 which stated, 'Women are making a speciality of decoration not merely because their adaptability makes them manipulate the new condition with greater facility than men, but also because decorative pen work is the legitimate descendent of embroidery and the purely feminine arts.'

Gradually, Newbery began to forge a Glasgow style which followed Ruskin's and Morris's belief that a work of art was whatever resulted from truth to form, materials, design and decoration. He believed that, while functional perfection has its own beauty, lesser things could be made greater by beauty of ornament. He did not agree that handicrafts were a separate discipline or a less pure form of artistic endeavour. He wanted to provide a good artistic training for craftsmen, and a good training in craftsmanship for his artists. Consequently, horn mallets and chasing punches, casting rings and embroidery silks became as much a part of his students' armamentaria as charcoal and paper.

Newbery was a convinced socialist. He organised evening classes in painting, architecture, metalwork and stained glass to further the education and training of the working class. He encouraged contacts with William Morris, Walter Crane, Arthur Gaskin and other supporters of Arts and Crafts principles. He supported workers' societies and tried to make them recognise their origins in the guilds of the past by means of lectures and occasional pageants and masques. He worked at his beliefs with missionary zeal and his results were astonishing. Within a decade the Glasgow School of Art had become, next to Birmingham, the most important art school in Britain.

10
'Pelleas et Melisande', pen and ink, 30.5 cm. × 13.3 cm., circa 1899. Fine Art Society

Jessie M. King came to Glasgow with nothing but a talent for drawing and an ability to record with commendable accuracy what her eye saw and what her mind could invent. She knew little of the history of art and even less of contemporary trends. The controversy that raged between the proponents of fine and applied art meant nothing to an artistically naïve young lady whose sensibilities were not far removed from chalking decorations on the flagged stone floors of the dairy or the tombstones in Bearsden churchyard. Newbery recognised the talent and saw the potential. He would teach her skills, aesthetics and principles. All he asked in exchange was diligence, perseverance and imagination, and these Jessie had in abundance.

Tuition at the school cost a modest £10 a year and, although the students had to pay for their own drawing materials, there were scholarships to be won throughout the course for the more talented. Money prizes were awarded at the local competitions and, each year, travelling scholarships were offered, with the most important one, the Haldane, allowing the successful student to explore in depth a number of art centres on the Continent. The working year consisted of only two terms. From June onwards the students were free to follow whatever pursuits they desired provided they participated in the Vacation Sketching Scheme. This consisted of projects set by the heads of departments to be worked on during the holidays. At the beginning of each new academic year the results were assessed and exhibited to the public. The judging and exhibiting of the finished work was done by the committee of the Glasgow School of Art Club, a body made up of former pupils, members of staff and external examiners all working under Newbery's direction. Newbery had also instituted monthly 'crits' to keep his students alert and to encourage every branch of the school's activities. Each July the best works were entered for the National Competition in South Kensington where medals and book prizes were awarded for distinguished work in painting, ornament, illustration, printing, poster work and other aspects of design.

Jessie began her training by being taught to draw from plaster casts. The cast room was small and filled with plaster heads, feet, arms, torsos and whole life-sized figures of Greek and Roman gods and heroes, each one on a plinth with castors to wheel it into position. The male students stood at their easels in suits and wing collars. The women, for the most part, wore smocks over their waisted jackets and blouses and ankle-length skirts. The tutors were dressed equally correctly in dark suits, their cuffs showing and handkerchiefs displayed in the breast pockets of their jackets. They stood around the class as dignified observers and advisers. Newbery would allow none of the wild dress and slovenliness of the notorious French academies. The two daily classes and the evening ones were meant to be attended promptly and unfailingly in the proper dress. Jessie's closest friend at the school was Helen Paxton Brown, a Glasgow girl of her own age. Nell Brown, in contrast to Jessie, was tall and dark with an almost Mediterranean beauty and had, like her friend, a fresh wit and a droll sense of humour. She was more placid than Jessie and a foil for her exuberant high spirits but she had a sweetness of nature that harmonised with Jessie's more volatile temperament. She wanted to be a painter but she was also a talented needlewoman, sufficiently so to be appointed, while she was still a student, demonstrator to

11 Helen Paxton Brown dressed for the Scottish National Pageant, 1908.

12 The Life Class at the Glasgow School of Art, circa 1899.

one of the Saturday morning classes for schoolteachers. Nell and Jessie spent their time at school in each other's company and went cycling around the Lanarkshire countryside at weekends and on holidays sketching the landscape. Jessie's sketchbooks of the time show her feeling her way with her drawings. They contained factual records of whatever caught her eye: an organ-grinder with his monkey; a child at play; boats in Stonehaven harbour; a church at Culross; ladies in crisp blouses, long skirts and boaters; and hills and cottages and sheep everywhere.

It soon became evident at school that Jessie's strength lay in imaginative line drawing. The basic course in Drawing from the Antique and Elementary Perspective was compulsory but, for some time, Jessie found it difficult to translate the intricacies of perspective onto paper. She worked by synthesis rather than analysis, building up her works unit by unit rather than dissecting them plane by plane. Her creations emerged by growth where other students' were hewn. Each summer the year's work was examined and the results announced as first or second class. Third class, which was tantamount to failure, was never mentioned in the published results. At the end of her first year Jessie received First Class grades in Advanced Drawing in Light and Shade, Advanced Model Drawing, Advanced Freehand Drawing, and a Second Class grade in Elementary Design. Her progress, though, was not uniformly good. Alongside these praiseworthy results there was a disturbing lack of mention in the pass list of her Perspective Drawing and Drawing from Memory. The weaknesses had to be corrected. Although she was allowed to move on into the second year studies it was on condition that she attend the first year classes again in her two failed subjects and resit the examinations.

13 *Jessie M. King aged nineteen, 1895.*

· CHAPTER THREE ·

Art Nouveau and the Stylists

Jessie M. King joined the Glasgow School of Art at a time when the orthodox Arts and Crafts principles had begun to be challenged by the heretical concepts of continental Art Nouveau. Walter Crane, C. R. Ashbee and the other leaders of the Arts and Crafts movement considered this new decorative style an effete and narcissistic parasite on their own muscular honesty. To them, decoration should arise out of form, not be superimposed on it. The classical nature of Arts and Crafts implied symmetry and stability; Art Nouveau, by its asymmetry, suggested movement and hence instability. Newbery, though, accepted Art Nouveau as a feature of artistic evolution and, in his teachings, attempted to reconcile the two, superimposing fluidity over a static core, so that the distinctly Scottish version of Art Nouveau, compared with its continental counterpart, became more rectilinear and structured.

The arrival of Art Nouveau was forcefully announced in April 1893 in the first number of *The Studio*. Subtitled 'A Magazine of the Applied Arts', *The Studio* proclaimed the importance of crafted objects and their ornament. From the beginning it recognised the changes that were taking place in decoration with the emergence of Art Nouveau and its practitioners. Rarely can an article of such devastating effect have opened in so diffident a manner as Joseph Pennel's evaluation in that opening issue of the work of the twenty-one-year-old Aubrey Beardsley. 'I have lately seen', he wrote, 'a few drawings that seem to me to be very remarkable.' The discovery of Beardsley jolted artistic sensibilities and forced a re-examination of traditional approaches to decorative art. Pennel remarked on Beardsley's links with both Japanese art and the Gothic woodcuts of the fifteenth century. He praised the beauty of his line and the rich strength of his black and white work. Nobody could ignore Beardsley's highly individual drawings. To young artists everywhere, the audacity of his vision countenanced a rebellion against formal academicism. He could outdo the French in 'depravity', and was looked on by his elders as a satanic emissary from a world filled with nightmare and decadent fantasy. He became a 'model' for several generations of illustrators. Glasgow students were affected by his innovations and began to rethink their own work. Jessie learned how a line might be made more seductive by fragmentation, how a mere procession of dots could be brought to a crescendo or a diminuendo, and how unmodelled and unpatterned shapes could be balanced by using only the weight of black and white masses.

The article on Beardsley, and a commentary in an issue later that year on the Dutch Symbolist painter Jan Toorop, helped to clarify the still uncertain artistic feelings of a young part-time student at the school, Charles Rennie Mackintosh. In 1890, he and Herbert MacNair, a colleague from the firm of architects Honeyman & Keppie where they were both employed as draughtsmen, began to attend evening classes in painting and drawing at the Glasgow School of Art. Both young men were interested in the mystical world of the Symbolists, a loose term which described many different styles of a subjective nature, and included the work of such varied painters as Gustav Moreau, Gauguin, Toorop and, nearer home, George Henry, E. A. Hornel, E. A. Walton, John Lavery and certain others of the 'Glasgow Boys'. In 1892, a year before *The Studio* illustrated Toorop's drawing *The Three Brides*, whose 'fantastic spirit of design', as the critic Walter Shaw Sparrow called it, was to have an important influence on the Glasgow Style, Mackintosh had already done a watercolour of a similar ghoulish vision entitled 'The Harvest Moon'. MacNair began to use equivalent themes and Fra Newbery noticed that two of his full-time students, the sisters Margaret and Frances Macdonald, were also working in the same ghostly style. 'The Four', as they came to be known, found that their symbolism was not just the outcome of their youthful need to be different but already the language of acknowledged masters. From the morbidity of their imagery the four artists became known half-derisively, half-affectionately as 'The Spooks', and Newbery showed their work as a group in the autumn of 1896 at an exhibition of the Glasgow School of Art Club where it was received with a mixed response.

The watercolours of 'The Spooks' were essentially figurative, but their content was unsubstantial and their structure often flaccid. Their mists and moonlight belonged to the later stages of Gothic romanticism. Their ectoplasmic forms, sometimes encased in bubbles like a developing embryo, sometimes with hair flowing out in skeins which, like that of Toorop's brides, merged with the surrounding trees, streams or sky, inhabited a land suspended between life and death where the occult and the secrets of eternity stood revealed. The swirls and tendrils were the stuff of Art Nouveau but, whereas Continental Art Nouveau was based on succulent plant forms, the new Celtic version used these strange humanoid figures as the basis for design. As other Glasgow students, including Jessie M. King herself, took up the artistic language of 'The Spooks', the elongated robed figures were bent to form abstract ornamental motifs looking like baskets or cressets or shields of finely wrought iron. Different artists: Agnes Harvey, DeCourcy Lewthwaite Dewar, Dorothy Smyth and Ann Macbeth among them, modelled them in relief in gesso, beat them into repoussé forms on thin sheets of metal, cast them as jewellery, used them as designs for posters or book covers, or displayed them in their own right as cabinet drawings and watercolours.

Each of 'The Four', whether by original inspiration or judicious borrowing, contributed to a common pool of iconography. The most popular motif was the large cabbage rose. Beardsley had already used it as a symbol of decadence and over-ripeness. The Glasgow artists used it more functionally as an island of rest in a design: a punctuation point in the eye's progress. They trained vertical plant forms on trellises, just as they had seen them in the work of the Pre-Raphaelites and, more significantly, in Beardsley's illustrations for *Salomé*. They borrowed swallows and lovebirds from William Morris,

14 Jan Toorop, 'The Three Brides', circa
1893. Watercolour, 78 cm. × 98 cm.
Rijksmuseum Kröller-Müller, Holland.

15 Charles Rennie
Mackintosh, 'The Harvest
Moon', 1892. Watercolour,
35.5 cm. × 28 cm. Glasgow
School of Art.

Charles Voysey and Talwin Morris who had come up to Glasgow from London as Blackie's chief book designer, and used them either in pairs supporting the sides of an object, where the hysteresis curve of their bodies made them ideal symbols of Art Nouveau, or in flocks swooping across a design to form contrasting horizontals with the main vertical axis. Although Mackintosh worked in the same idiom as his fellow 'Spooks' his sense of form made him ill-at-ease with their structural vagueness. It was his insertion of a 'backbone' that gave the Glasgow Style individuality and influence. In France, Belgium and Italy, Art Nouveau developed as an extrovert, nervous and dynamic form of expression. Its shapes were open-ended and spread

16
Jessie M. King, 'Wynken,
Blynken and Nod', circa
1899. Pen and ink.

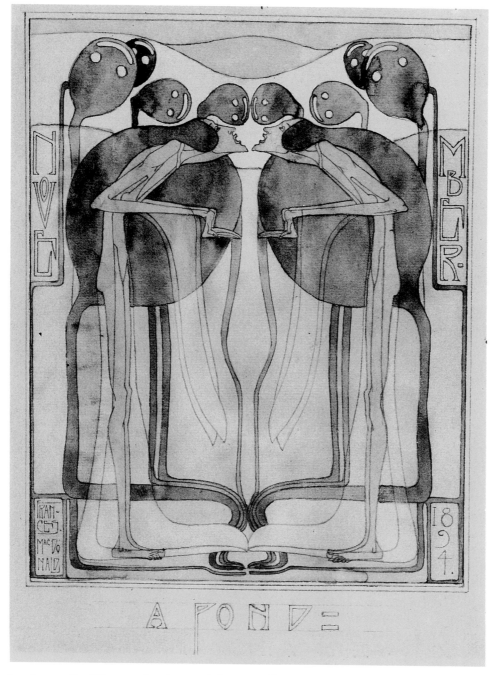

17
Frances Macdonald, 'A Pond', 1894. Watercolour. Glasgow School of Art

horizontally. They twined round designs, flowing and writhing sensually, and then suddenly lashed back on themselves in a totally unexpected way. The Glasgow Style, which grew partly out of 'Spook' forms, was mainly vertical in structure. Its human and vegetable shapes tended to spread up and down a surface rather than across it. As plants grew upwards from the bottom, hair flowed downwards from the top. The Glasgow forms were often enclosed in geometrical casings of grid-like structures, ellipses or heart shapes, that made them very different from the often fussy, anarchical forms of Horta in Belgium or Gallé and Majorelle in France (see plates 16, 17, 18, 28, 29, 31).

The Studio recognised the significance of the new Glasgow Style and, through its efforts, Glasgow came to be respected as a centre of design throughout Europe, especially in Austria and Germany. In November 1898 the magazine *Dekorative Kunst*, published by Alexander Koch in Darmstadt, took up the cause of the Glasgow School and praised the work of 'The Four' and of Mackintosh in particular. Hermann Muthesius, in his book *Das Englische Haus* in 1904 declared, 'The Scottish movement is a reaction against the insistent utilitarianism and rational principles of the Arts and Crafts camp in London. They preached death to romanticism and were thinking mainly of the stylistic chaos, the meaningless ornament and the forgotten consideration of material and craftsmanship that marked the end of the nineteenth century. The Scots replied that without imagination there is no art.'

The Celtic mysticism of 'The Four' and the manner in which they expressed it had a special meaning for Jessie M. King. At the age of sixteen before she had started art school she had undergone what she sincerely believed to have been a psychic experience. She had been lying on the grass in a field one summer, perhaps dozing, and had felt a pricking sensation on her eyelids. She was convinced that this was a deliberate action by the 'Little People' to single her out as a communicant between their world and hers. However much a later, more cynical, judgement might deride such an interpretation of what might have been an insect alighting on Jessie's face, it should perhaps be remembered that 1891 was a time when the recently-formed Society for Psychical Research was active, and such terms as 'the other world' and 'ectoplasm' were topics for serious discussion. Not only could the touch of 'Little People' seem reasonable to a romantic schoolgirl but the very imagery of 'The Spooks' might well have been based on similar occult beliefs. Jessie maintained that from then onwards she was blessed with second sight. She felt that she had been 'selected', and she adduced various instances of successful prediction of future events to support her claim. She suddenly found herself able to draw lines of an unbelievable fineness and, whether or not this coincided with the discovery that she was myopic, so that close things were magnified, she attributed this to the gift of the 'Little People'. Jessie M. King was neither fey nor a charlatan. She was not a fool and was not easily beguiled. Like most people she had her eccentricities, some of which she traded on as social capital. However, she had been brought up by Mary McNab who was practical and down-to-earth in matters relating to the running of a home but who also, beneath her religious discipline, remained a country-woman and bore the legacy of an ancient Celtic tradition with its echoes of paganism and superstition. The intimacy between Jessie and Maime must have allowed folk legend and Christian belief to mingle in Jessie's mind from an early and impressionable age, and the results dictated the unique response in her work to any dramatic stimulus. Jessie looked upon her ability to draw in microscopic detail as a favour and a blessing, to be set apart from what she was being taught at art school and to be used in private.

In a later article on her work in *The Booklovers' Magazine*, 1908, using a prose style as much related to the Celtic twilight as anything in Jessie's drawings, E. A. Taylor wrote, 'It is to the bank of fancy we must go to find Miss King: where the pebbles dot over the shore, the butterfly shells whisper

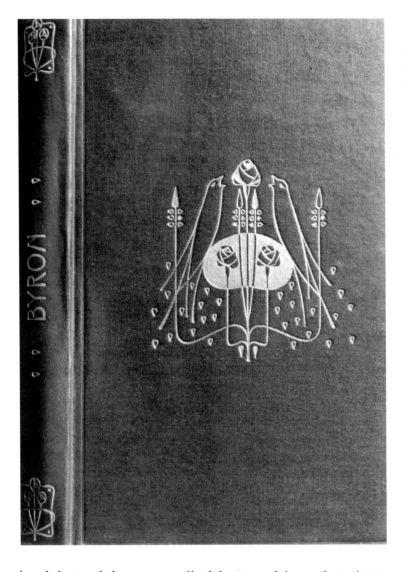

18
*Talwyn Morris, cover
design for* Poems by Byron,
*published by Blackie and
Sons, 1908.*

of the sea beyond and the sand-dune roses tell of the joys of the surf wind.' He conceded that 'some of the marks' Jessie made might have originated with Beardsley, but insisted that she should not be looked upon as one of his followers. He described Beardsley's drawings as 'touching a beautiful soulless melody', but Jessie's as 'a beautiful melody of soul'. He called her 'the poet's artist, dipping down behind the veil to discover poetry in the actual, and an ideal in the real'.

In the work of 'The Four' Jessie found images that were not unlike those of her own secret world. Hers, though, were less menacing than those of 'The Spooks'. Theirs pictured Shades, loss of hope and the dank emptiness that lay beyond the grave. Hers spoke of redemption, beauty and fulfilment. Both types of artistic expression were manifestations of the Symbolist movement in art. They were related in that both were attempting to record an inner world of escapism by means of fantasy. Although the 'Spook School' dispersed and its members developed by going their separate ways, all the artists who had shared its visions retained some echo of its mystical origins in their later work.

· CHAPTER FOUR ·

Days of Change

Jessie M. King was younger than 'The Four' and, during the evolutionary years of the Glasgow Style, was struggling with technical rather than stylistic matters. In 1894, at the end of her second year, she was awarded first prize in the Local Examinations for the design of a plate in the unusual medium of stained glass. More academically, she also won a prize for a group of anatomy studies. She obtained First-Class grades in Advanced Model Drawing, Advanced Freehand Drawing and Advanced Drawing in Light and Shade. She even scraped a pass in Elementary Perspective. It was a good year.

Her achievements at school, though, were overshadowed by events at home. On 18 September Graham, Jessie's young brother, died of tuberculosis at the age of eighteen. As the baby of the family, and the only boy, he had been petted and cosseted by them all. For some time, as the disease progressed, he had needed a stick to walk with, and a photograph taken shortly before he died shows him coming to terms with the inevitability of death. He was buried in the churchyard across the road from his home. Jessie returned to school a fortnight later, still shocked and wearing her statutory black.

She repeated her previous year's successes at the school in 1895 and again won a prize for a glass design, but Newbery could see that her talents inclined toward the literary. He appreciated her sensitivity within what was really a somewhat limited range. He was wise enough to realise that to mould Jessie's natural gifts into the routine discipline of a set curriculum might inhibit an individual creative urge. Consequently, at the beginning of the autumn term he excused her a year's attendance at some of the formal classes in order to let her concentrate on illustration and design. He knew that in doing so he was allowing Jessie to abandon the Diploma course and her commitment to becoming a teacher.

Jessie's joy in her freedom was tempered with a sense of guilt that came with the sudden death of her mother. Jessie's parents, grieving at the loss of their only son and bearer of the family name, had determined to have another child in the hope that it might be a boy. In the event, Mary King, who was then fifty, died giving birth to a stillborn child on 1 May 1896. The girls spent the summer together replanning the household. Eva and Maime were to run the home. Peggy was to become her father's secretary and be in charge of the household and parish accounts. Jessie was allowed to return to school in September knowing that her father's needs were being safely looked after. She had used her year to consolidate her understanding of the art of illustration. When school started again she returned to the normal curriculum with her ideas clarified and her technique much more assured.

Writing to her many years later in 1921 and addressing her as 'Dear friend, colleague and consoeur', Fra Newbery reminisced about those days. He recalled how Jessie, as a student, was somewhat overweight. 'You needed a little banting,' he suggested, and reminded her of the journey she made each day from Bearsden to what he called 'those dear, dirty rooms in Rose Street'. He remembered Jessie's fire and enthusiasm, 'though not,' he recalled, 'for the studies from the antique, in those days when food and drink were unimportant time-wasting activities, when there was art to be created and the spirit was alive.' He felt that the very difficulties of the surroundings provided their own stimulus and that the move later to the comparative luxury of the new School building had made the students soft and had weakened their spirit. 'Nothing like starving an artist to get the best out of him,' he wrote, signing himself 'Your old friend and fellow worker, Fra Newbery'.

The academic year 1896–7 was Jessie's best at the School. She attended all the required classes: Life, Anatomy, Drawing from Memory and Still Life. She drew drapery and designed fabrics, studied ornament and produced decorative designs in various media. At the end of the school year, with First-Class grades in most of her subjects, she was awarded the important Queen's Prize for her work on Principles of Ornament. She also received a National Book Prize from South Kensington for three designs for a nursery frieze based on scenes and characters from Kipling's *Jungle Book*. She won a prize of 7s 6d for a study of drapery and one of 10s for an interior decoration. She was also granted a Free Studentship for the coming year with the possibility of an extension if her progress continued to be satisfactory.

In her last year as a student Jessie was allowed to concentrate on book decoration and illustration. She obtained a 'First' with honours for examples of bookbinding, cover designs, page decoration and illustration. In June she again received the Queen's Prize and the examiners expressed their 'great admiration' of her entry. More significantly, because it received international coverage in *The Studio*, she was awarded a Silver Medal in the National Competition for a group of eight illustrations of scenes from Sir Edwin Arnold's epic poem 'The Light of Asia' which told, in a style not unlike Tennyson's popular 'Idylls of the King', the story of Prince Siddhartha and how he became the Buddha. The examiners, who included Walter Crane, the newly elected President of the Royal College of Art, summed up their decision to award Jessie the prize by describing her entry as 'a remarkable set of designs distinguished by fine ornamental feeling expressed in a new way'. But in case it was felt that their praise was lacking in critical acumen, they added 'The excessive attenuation of her figures, however, mars her work which otherwise might have obtained a higher award'. The examiners were no doubt impressed by the way the illustrations conformed to Arts and Crafts principles by using forms of an almost Grecian simplicity in a decorative manner. The attenuation of her figures was a deliberate attempt to let the drawings, done without shading and in pure outline, match the universality of the message.

Her 'The Light of Asia' drawings were remarkably mature for so young a person and they contained many elements that Jessie was to elaborate on in

her later work. They were all horizontal in format and each one included a narrow panel of quotation at the side. The lettering was done in a manner that was becoming characteristic of the students at the Glasgow School. It had been introduced by Jessie Rowat, one of Fra Newbery's first pupils and later his wife, into her needlework designs. She took as specimens the letters on seventeenth-century Scottish plaques and tombstones, and worked them into her patterns in the way they had done in medieval times. Their use spread beyond her needlework classes and they became one of the features of the Glasgow Style. The letters were based on Roman forms but were more 'leggy', with high cross-bars on 'E', 'F' and 'A'. Everybody devised their own variations on the basic forms and Jessie King eventually made a personal feature of separating each letter from its fellows by a dot or a star. In her 'The Light of Asia' drawings she included as additional decoration beneath the text some of the little squares that Mackintosh liked to use and which, when the Glasgow Style became famous, were taken up to great effect by Josef Hoffmann and the other Austrian Secessionists.

All eight drawings had shallow perspective, and each one showed a bank of cloud made up of horizontal strands similar to the hair of Toorop's *The Three Brides*. Mackintosh, too, built up skies in this way in some of his architectural drawings, and 'The Spooks' used them as hanging banks of mist to add mystery to a scene. Jessie M. King used them structurally as a second horizon so that, with the ground low down and the figures viewed from below, the pictures seemed strangely ambiguous. She drew the figures in profile and stressed the vertical elements by introducing trees and bushes to frame the scene. This resulted in a grid-like structure, not unlike a noughts-and-crosses framework or even a tartan, which Jessie found so versatile that she incorporated it, time and again in her works (see plates 21, 46, 51, 58, 84). There were strong links, too, with Arts and Crafts practice in the little arcs of

MDCXXXIV

COMVS·A·MASKE

BY·JOHN·MILTON

ILLVSTRATED·BY·JESSIE·M·KING
GEORGE·ROVTLEDGE·AND·SONS·LTD
LONDON:·BROADWAY·HOVSE·LVDGATE·HILL·E

21
*Jessie M. King, title page
for* Comus, *published by
Routledge, 1905.*

stylised flowers that she set on either side of some of the characters in order to
balance and formalise the figures.

'The Light of Asia' drawings contained other motifs that had become the common property of the Glasgow students. Stylised, lancet-shaped leaves, like those of the Bodi tree under which the Buddha received his enlightenment, rose in vertical clusters on stems, often collected into fasces, which curled across the picture and made the upright leaves look like so many sparrows on a clothes line. These spear-like bundles appeared in many forms in the work of the Glasgow Stylists. Ann Macbeth used them in her embroideries, Mackintosh used them in his ironwork on the Glasgow School of Art building and in his posters, and they appeared as plinths, capitals and coronets in Jessie's works. In another variation, Jessie made a bowed rectangle out of the shape and used it to frame the head of a saint, or as a finial or a cresset, in her book decorations (see plates 29, 30, 32, 47). She drew haloes around the heads of many of the living creatures in the series to signify their life force. Mackintosh and the Macdonald sisters had often bound their wiry figures with loops and circles like the orbits of some fantastic planetary system. Jessie elaborated on these, making the haloes more numerous and more complex in pattern so that, in time, she would have as many as five loops swirling about her figures, each one made up of trails of stars or petals, or rings of the finest dots. She gave Buddha himself a different halo in each of the drawings: one of lotus buds, another of swallows, to symbolise the idea of the unity of all living things that was at the heart of his teaching.

'The Light of Asia' drawings were seen by Gleeson White, the editor of *The Studio*, who was impressed by their sincerity. In an article in the magazine in which three of the drawings were reproduced he wrote:

> The treatment lifts the incidents she has chosen to represent out of the commonplace and invests them with a dignity befitting the subject of the poem. While the figure is idealised it is drawn with a knowledge of form and a refinement of line that disarms criticism and commands admiration . . . The designs generally appear to us to reveal much artistic power and feeling; whilst they are representative of the tendencies of this younger school and share its conventionalism and symbolism, there is, withal, a sweetness not often allied with work so abstracted and idealised in character.

White kept up his interest in Jessie M. King's progress, and *The Studio* made regular mention of her in articles, studio notes and illustrations of her work. Jessie M. King's international fame may be said to have come about as much through the magazine's support as through Newbery's promotion of her talents. It raises again the question of whether an inspired teacher can be the agent of change or whether that change is the inevitable movement of an unending progress, with the teacher as the co-ordinator who happens to be there at the time. The list of Jessie M. King's contemporaries at the Glasgow School of Art reads like an index of Scottish Art Nouveau. Either together, or overlapping by a very few years, were the extraordinary talents of Jessie Rowat, Frances and Margaret Macdonald, Herbert MacNair, Charles Rennie Mackintosh, Ann Macbeth, Helen Paxton Brown, DeCourcy Lewthwaite Dewar, Agnes Harvey, Annie French and Katherine Cameron. Between them they secured a place for the Glasgow Style in the history of art.

22 Jessie M. King, 'Siddartha Laid the Bird's Neck beside his own Cheek', from The Light of Asia; *pen and ink, 1898.*

Like all successful teachers, Fra Newbery attracted disciples and, as news of the work being done at Glasgow spread, the number of applications to join the school increased. Space and facilities at Rose Street were limited and hampered Newbery's plans to expand his courses. He needed new and larger premises with greater classroom accommodation and better lighting. The Board of Governors, to their credit, were sympathetic to his arguments and offered a site in Renfrew Street albeit with a budget that fell far short of Newbery's expectations. A small competition was held and the firm of Honeyman and Keppie submitted plans drawn up, possibly at Newbery's suggestion, by the young Mackintosh, who was on their staff. Mackintosh's design was selected and it was envisaged that, because of the financial restrictions, the building should take place in two phases.

The site was an architect's nightmare with a long axis on the crest of a hill and the shorter side running down the slope of an even steeper one, like a chimney on a rooftop. Mackintosh's genius produced a building that has become a landmark in early twentieth-century European architecture, and, despite differences in influence and philosophy, as important to the history of Art Nouveau as Gaudi's Sagrada Familia in Barcelona. It was planned by an artist for artists to work in and enjoy. The rooms and studios were designed to flow into one another and utilise space and light in the best possible way. The decorative niceties of little squares of purple glass let into the doors and light fittings, and the wrought-iron knots, not unlike Jessie M. King's rose briars, reflected Mackintosh's interest in symbols and shapes and brought charm and grace to otherwise functional objects.

The foundation stone was laid on 25 May 1898 in a ceremony conducted by Sir Rennie Watson the Lord Provost attended by the City Council, the magistrature, the police and clergy, as well as Fra Newbery, members of his staff and Jessie M. King who was there in a special capacity. Mackintosh, although present, was not named as architect in either the newspaper reports or the Annual Report of the Board of Governors because he was not then a partner in the firm of Honeyman and Keppie. Jessie was invited because Newbery had asked her to prepare an illuminated history of the School in pen, ink and watercolour, embellished with silver and gold. The vellum scroll, described in the reports as 'chief among the documents', was placed in the cavity of the foundation stone, only to be lost, it would seem, for ever, because nobody bothered to make a record of which stone was the actual one consecrated.

That December, when Jessie was at home celebrating Christmas, her father suffered a heart attack. By the time his doctor could be contacted the Revd King had died. His death completely altered the lives of his daughters. The Manse, being church property, was needed for the next incumbent. The livestock, apart from Jessie's precious rabbits, had to be sold, and Jessie went to live with Mary in a cottage they found for her in the village of Milton of Campsie, not far from Bearsden. Jessie had always felt closer to her father than to her mother. She admired his wisdom and his sense of justice. His remoteness, his gravity and his moments of severity went with his calling, but his innate goodness of nature was never withheld from his family or his parishioners. He had always been protected from the day-to-day trivialities by his cohort of women but he was not able, as he had hoped, to officiate at the wedding of any one of them. Ironically, on the very day of his death, he had learned that Jessie had sold her first picture for the handsome sum of £5.

Travelling from Mary's cottage to the School of Art was difficult and Jessie began to look for accommodation in Glasgow itself. She and Nell Brown discovered a block of newly converted studio flats at the top of an insurance building at 101 St Vincent Street. There were five flights of stairs but the reward was a magnificent view over the city, an excellent north light and the fact that the School was only a few minutes' walk away. They rented adjacent flats and were to live there for the next nine years.

A year after moving in the girls were joined in a third flat by their friend Archie Taylor. Ernest Archibald Taylor was born on 5 September 1874 at Greenock where his father, Major William Edward Taylor of the Royal Garrison Artillery, was in charge of Fort-Matilda, then an army barracks but originally established to defend the Clyde during the Napoleonic wars. Archie was the fifteenth of what were to be seventeen children, a fact which, from an early age, he made every effort to conceal. His mother, Frances Hawkins, came from Newfoundland and, after her marriage, travelled from posting to posting with her husband and their ever-increasing family. Because of their itinerant upbringing the Taylor children had no settled roots. Every two years or so, in the course of army transfer, there was a disruption as the family moved to a new town or country. New friendships had to be made and a new life started. It was not altogether surprising then that the Taylor children were fairly cosmopolitan, and that when they left home they spread themselves throughout the world. Three of Archie's sisters lived in Chicago, a brother lived in Demerara in British Guiana and another brother, Bob, after an adventurous life in Central America and the United States, ended up as a

23 *E. A. Taylor aged twenty, 1894.*

shipping broker in Cuba. Archie's favourite sister, Kate, lived in Scotland, and it was Scotland that remained the mother country to all the Taylors, no matter where they settled.

In 1880, when Major Taylor had been posted to East Deering in Norfolk, an offer came from a brother living in Greenock for young Archie to come and live with him. Uncle and nephew were already good friends and the child moved into his new home without difficulty. He was sent to the Highlanders Academy, an elementary school in the town, and from there, at the age of ten, went to a private school, Greenock Academy. The benevolent uncle had promised to bring up Archie as his heir but, when the boy was in his late teens the uncle married a young wife who resented Archie's presence and influence with her husband. In the ensuing tensions Archie was forced to leave home and move into lodgings.

Now calling himself Ernest rather than the less dignified Archie he signed forms for training as an apprentice engineering designer with the shipbuilding firm of Scott & Co. at their Greenock Foundry. At seventeen he was a well-proportioned young man, not over-tall, with a gaunt expressive face and an aquiline nose. He carried himself well and was attractive in both person and personality. His great passion, as strong even as his artistic leanings, was for the theatre. He had a pleasing voice, both speaking and singing, he read widely and acted well in amateur productions. He had a large repertoire of poetry that he had committed to memory, and was in demand for his skill as a reciter of poems and humorous monologues.

E. A. Taylor had drawn and sketched since childhood and, on completing his apprenticeship in October 1896, began to think seriously about taking up painting. He had met Charles Rennie Mackintosh one summer when they were both on sketching holidays on Arran and had been greatly impressed by Mackintosh's method of working. He later said that it was from that first meeting that he had learned the difference between seeing and perceiving. Taylor stayed on at the foundry as a draughtsman designer for a further two years and left amicably in July 1898 to take up a post as designer for Wylie & Lochhead, the Glasgow firm of house furnishers and decorators. He took with him a flattering testimonial recommending his versatility and talent, 'particularly where work of an artistic kind is required'. He hoped that by working in Glasgow he would be able to enrol for painting classes at the School of Art but, before he could take up his new post he developed osteomyelitis of the leg and was admitted to the Western Infirmary at Glasgow for an operation. The long convalescence that followed set back his plans, and the residual focus of infection which, in those days could not be fully eradicated without amputation, left him with a recurrent abscess that affected him for the rest of his life.

Wylie and Lochhead were adventurous in their designs and occupied a position in Glasgow equivalent to Liberty's or Heal's in London. Taylor became part of an excellent team, which included George Logan and John Ednie, and, together they produced original modern designs for chairs, cabinets, tables, fireplace surrounds, decorative panels in various media and the general décor for complete rooms.

Through his colleagues at Wylie's, and the friends he made at the evening classes at the School of Art, Taylor got to know the work of the new exponents of the new Glasgow Style. He mixed with them socially and, as someone who already had practical experience of designing for industry, was listened to as an authority. He became part of the group that included Nell Brown and Jessie King, and a special relationship built up between the laughing extrovert 'Jake', as he called her, and the handsome, sophisticated and popular young man. He had proposed marriage to her a few weeks before her father died and the Revd King had given his consent. Ernest presented Jessie with a ring he had designed himself and had made up by a local jeweller. There was no question of an early wedding. Ernest was unable to support a wife and, in any case, was reluctant to give up the joys of this new art world where his obvious charm made him popular with both sexes. The engagement was prolonged and not until 1908, when he was committed to leaving Glasgow for a new job in Salford, did Ernest and Jessie take the decisive step.

· CHAPTER FIVE ·

Continental Acclaim

Jessie M. King's work began to attract attention. In February 1899 one of her illustrations was shown at the inaugural exhibition of the Scottish Society of Art Workers. More significantly, that summer, two of her drawings were selected for exhibition at the Venice Biennale: one, a design for a diploma certificate which, together with a school badge, she had been asked to do for the Glasgow School of Art; the other was one of two versions she illustrated of the 'Tower' scene from Maeterlinck's 'Pelleas and Melisande' (plate 10). In the National Competition she was again awarded a Silver Medal, this time for a group of illustrations of incidents from William Morris's story 'The Wood Beyond the World', and was further honoured by having three of them reproduced in *The Studio*.

The new drawings were similar in format to her 'The Light of Asia' series and used many of the same motifs. The figures were again two-dimensional in appearance and had the same unworldly look as those earlier ones, but their haloes of stars, and chains of flowers were more elaborate, often continuing as garlands around the filmy ankle-length dresses of the maidens and building up on the ground as a thick carpet. A fairy ship with a high poop and billowing sails, strewn with petals and tinkling bells, lay at anchor, totally unseaworthy in appearance but then, on the oceans on which it was to sail, there were no storms or shipwrecks. The ship of dreams was to appear many times again in Jessie's work and already, even in these school drawings, there could be seen her interest in realities of another order of existence, with rules which bore only a tenuous connection to everyday life. In their solemn-faced report on the award, the examiners, who included Linley Sambourne, the illustrator of *The Water Babies*, declared that Jessie M. King 'has improved upon last year in the proportion of the figures introduced into her work, which still leaves something to be desired in that respect. She has, however, fallen into an unfortunate defect of spottiness, which mars the general breadth of some of her designs. The lettering is harmonious with the designs, and is fairly legible and original.' *The Studio*, less stuffily, made special mention of what it called 'the bright and original work of Jessie M. King', and praised her new drawings for their 'excellent imagination and fine sense of line and composition'.

In September 1899 Fra Newbery offered her a teaching post at the School in the Department of Book Decoration & Design under John Macbeth. She held the position at the same time as attending her last classes at the School and was delighted to be paid for doing what was, in effect, a continuation of

24
Jessie M. King, 'And they two passed by him', from 'The Wood beyond the World' by William Morris, 1899. Pen and ink.

25
Jessie M. King, binding for D. G. Rossetti's Ballads, 1899. Pen, ink and gilt on Vellum, 16.5 cm. × 12 cm. Robin de Beaumont collection

26
Opposite. Jessie M. King, Vellucent binding for The High History of the Holy Graal, *1903. Private collection.*

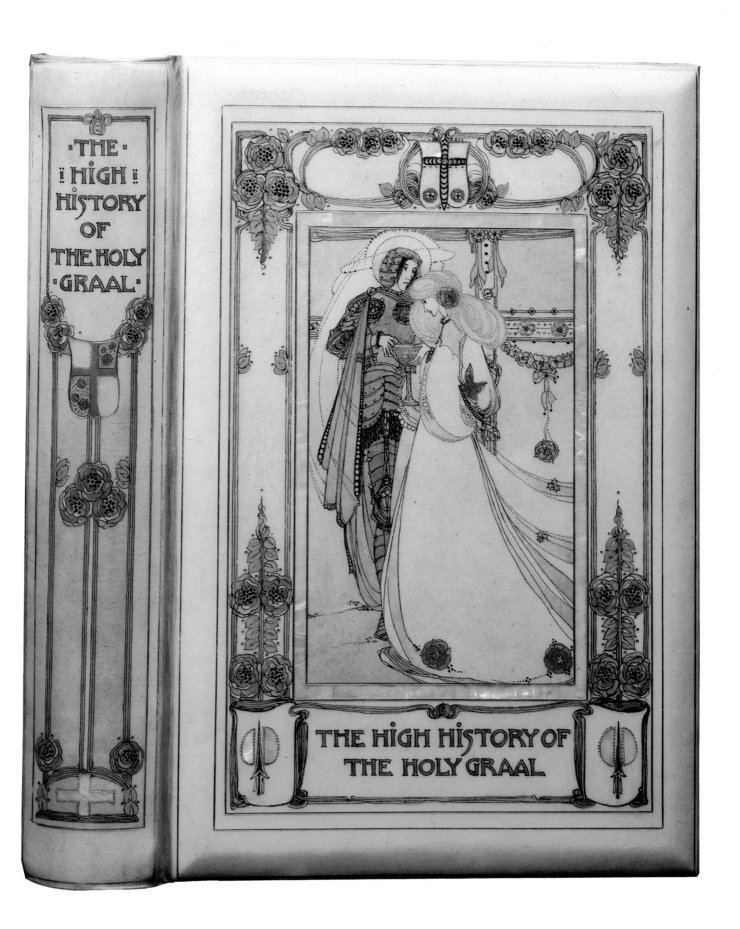

her School activities. Her work involved demonstrating the art of book binding and decoration, the use of ornament lettering, and illustration. She designed and bound examples for her class and worked on more elaborate specimens for crafting by professional binders such as MacLehose in Glasgow and Chivers in Bath. The simplest of these craftsman-bindings was done in limp vellum for a copy of Rossetti's *Ballads*. It consisted of a single sheet of vellum with an illustration in fine penwork covering the whole sheet and a central panel into which the pages were sewn with ribbons.

The most beautiful, and certainly the most ornate, of the bindings was done by Chivers in 1902 in what the firm called their Vellucent binding, for a copy of *The Story of Rosalynde*. Chivers had invented a process for treating vellum to make it translucent. The cover design was drawn or painted on a separate sheet that was applied to the vellum from underneath and the binding tooled from above. Jessie's design of knights in armour arranged about an immense rose tree was done in pen and ink with touches of lilac and pale green, and inlaid with thin slices of mother-of-pearl. There were two, almost identical, versions of the cover, but the fact that a knight on one had been given an unnecessarily prominent moustache seems to indicate that Jessie had been trying to hide an accidental blot. She did two other Vellucent designs for Chivers. One, which was in the style of the bent-wire abstract figures of the 'Spooks', was for a copy of *L'Evangile de l'Enfance*, a book about the disastrous Children's Crusade, and won her a Gold Medal at the Turin Exhibition of 1902. The other, in 1904, was an exquisite confection in pinks,

27 *Jessie M. King,* Vellucent binding for The Story of Rosalynde, *1902. Robin de Beaumont Collection.*

greens and yellows for a copy of *The High History of the Holy Graal* which she herself had illustrated.

Jessie M. King used the 'wirework figures' in only a very few of her works. They became the bases of the designs for a group of covers for a Berlin publisher in 1899; for a copy of Emile Zola's *Le Rêve* that was hand-bound by John Macbeth in 1900; for a superb bookplate for William Rowat, the father of Jessie Newbery, and lastly, in 1903 for the title page of 'The High History of the Holy Graal'. All the designs were figuratively based but were made so geometric that at first glance they seemed to be little more than abstract patterns of loops and parabolas, circles and elipses, with only the faces having a link with reality. Jessie drew several haloes spinning about the heads, sometimes doubled and set obliquely like the rings of Saturn. Some of the ovals and circles traced out the outlines of the figures, and each form was wrapped round with spirals like the binding on a mummy. The ghostly apparitions seemed to dissolve in the surrounding space, and the effect was to make their links with human substance even more tenuous. The logical outcome of this depersonalisation came in a cover that Jessie designed for a book of photographs *Rund um Berlin*, in which she used the elipses and inverted hearts very cleverly in a totally abstract manner with all the figure references abolished.

28
Jessie M. King, frontispiece for L'Evangile de l'Enfance, *circa 1900. Pen and ink on vellum.*

Rund um Berlin was part of Jessie's first large-scale commission. In 1899, Georg Wertheim, whose family owned a large department store in Berlin, had written to Fra Newbery asking for somebody to design for him in the new Scottish style. Newbery had recommended Jessie M. King and, although no evidence has come to light it has been suggested that she designed wallpaper, wrapping paper and various items of ephemera for the store. She also received commissions to design covers and endpapers for books to be published by Wertheim's associate firm Globus for sale in the store. The first was for a series of books of photographs of German cities and landmarks. Jessie sent Wertheim four designs. Taken as a sequence, with each one more refined down to abstraction than its predecessor, they represent an extraordinary achievement for so inexperienced an artist. The earliest one, stylistically, showed the same kneeling semi-abstract figures as those in the frontispiece of *L'Evangile de l'Enfance*, and was used for the cover of a book of photographs of Dresden and Saxon Switzerland. Proceeding from this, Jessie designed the cover for *Rund um Berlin*, which used 'Spook' shapes but eliminated all reference to faces or limbs so that only a devotee would know that the ellipses and hearts were once the embodiments of ghostly maidens and that the fusiform arcs were once flights of birds. Even more abstract was a third design which was used for *Album von Berlin* and was one of Jessie's most imaginative conceptions. Combining German orderliness with Scottish fantasy it set the Imperial Eagle in a framework of climbing rosebushes with clusters of petals stylised like so many iron crosses. Globus used the design again, with different lettering, for companion volumes on Frankfurt and on the monuments of

30
Jessie M. King, first version
of the cover design for
Album von Berlin, *1899.*
27.3 cm. × 34.3 cm.

31
Jessie M. King, second
version of the cover design
for Album von Berlin, *1899.*
27.3 cm. × 34.3 cm.

Berlin. The most figurative of Jessie's covers, which featured a young girl, was used for another edition of *Album von Berlin* and also appeared, despite its Germanic overtones, for an equivalent book of photographs of Edinburgh which Patrick Thomson's, a firm of house furnishers in the city, brought out.

The girl of the second *Album von Berlin* cover reappeared in different settings in two other designs Jessie did for Wertheim: an album of music entitled *Musik und Gesang*, for which she also did a beautiful endpaper with a

AND·GAVE·THE·NAKED·SHIELD·

32
Jessie M. King, 'And gave the naked shield', illustration for Elaine, Lord Tennyson, *published by Routledge 1903. Ink on vellum, 23.3 cm. × 19.1 cm. Hunterian Art Gallery, Glasgow.*

33
Jessie M. King, illustration for The Magic Grammar *by Oliver Gray, circa 1901. Pen and ink.*

fairy motif, and the first of a series of art books, *Werke Alter Meister*, which Globus published in 1902. The girl was always dressed in a high-waisted, ankle-length robe, with her hair in heavy coils held in place by a large full-blown rose behind the ear. Jessie introduced the Glasgow rose into many of her drawings. Mackintosh had used it on a curved stem as a decorative unit in painted stencils and stained glass. Jessie introduced it into the pattern of cloaks and dresses, as exotic mouldings on pillars and furniture and, most commonly, as an actual flower for adornment as Burne-Jones and Rossetti had done. She had a special gift of being able to visualise how this and other symbols could be changed into unexpected forms. In a drawing *The Magic Grammar*, for instance, she joined two of Mackintosh's curved roses together to make a heart. The hearts became maidens. Maidens became butterflies, and butterflies became banners in a display of prestidigitation that left the viewer breathless with admiration.

The maidens on the Globus covers were the prototypes of all the forlorn princesses that Jessie was ever to draw. Their faces, usually in profile or three-quarter view, were not always beautiful. The philtrum was too short and the lower jaw too prominent, like those of the Pre-Raphaelite women, Jane Morris and Elizabeth Siddal, who had inspired them. Jessie's princesses were attractive because they looked ingenuous and helpless, rather than arrogant in their beauty. Their feet and hands were always sensitively drawn. Their

34
Edward Burne-Jones, 'Going to the Battle', 1858. Pen and ink and wash on vellum, 22.5 cm. × 19.5 cm. Fitzwilliam Museum, Cambridge.

35
Sandro Botticelli, detail from 'La Primavera', late 1470's. Panel 203 cm. × 312.5 cm. Uffizzi Gallery, Florence.

36
Jessie M. King, 'The White Knight', 1902. Pen and ink on vellum.

fingers were long and tapering, with the first and fourth often splayed and the two middle ones in contact, adding to the gracefulness and, at the same time, perhaps unconsciously, making the sign to ward off Satan that the Irish artist Harry Clarke was to make a feature of a decade later. Jessie's maidens rarely wore shoes. They trod on the ground, or sometimes just above it, in bare feet, exactly as Botticelli's nymphs did in the reproduction of *La Primavera* that she owned. It was also *La Primavera*, as much as what she had seen in Beardsley's drawings, that moved Jessie to fill her pictures with petals blowing through the air like confetti, settling on the maidens' dresses or mingling with their haloes in swirls that rose upwards to become confused with the stars themselves.

Jessie M. King's binding for *L'Evangile de l'Enfance* was selected for display at the First International Exhibition of Modern Decorative Art that was held in Turin in 1902. Mackintosh and his colleagues had already demonstrated the vigour of the new Scottish School at the Vienna Secessionist Exhibition of 1900 and, on the strength of this, Fra Newbery had been invited to organise the Scottish entry at Turin. It was the first time that the Glasgow Style of decorative art had been displayed in all its variety, and the importance of the exhibition was underlined by the fact that the official opening on 10 May was by the King of Italy himself. Mackintosh was appointed by Newbery as architect and designer of the Scottish pavilion. He divided the allotted area into three rooms and decorated each one in the quiet colours that the members of the Glasgow Style had begun to use in reaction to the vivid peacock blues and sap greens of Morris, Crane and the Aesthetes. The first room, 'The Rose Boudoir', had furniture and decorated panels in gesso and beaten metal by Margaret Macdonald and Mackintosh himself. The central room was furnished as a writing room by Herbert MacNair and Frances Macdonald, and included examples of needlework by Jessie Newbery, Ann Macbeth and other members of the School. The third and largest room was devoted to objects done by School and non-School designers, and included a cabinet by E. A. Taylor done in silvered wood with an inset panel of stained glass, and a screen by George Logan which had one of Jessie's drawings *The Princess of the Red Rose* let into its central leaf. Other drawings by Jessie, done in her most wispy manner, were hung at intervals around the walls, and between them were panels of metalwork and needlework, and two of stained glass by E. A. Taylor. Down the middle of the floor were two long showcases with pieces in enamelwork, and jewellery in pewter, silver and gold done by the students.

Alongside these were books designed by Talwin Morris, and the copies of Christina Rossetti's *Poems* and *L'Evangile de l'Enfance* which won for Jessie her Gold Medal. She also received a certificate designed in a mixture of Art Nouveau styles which had three Mucha-like graces playing with a ribbon that spelt out ARS, surrounded by a network of very non-Glasgow briars, whilst below, in the type of Scottish lettering that had now become common in the Continental Art Nouveau world, a proclamation that 'Signor' Jessie M. King had been awarded this highest honour.

The Turin Exhibition was widely reported in Continental art magazines and Fra Newbery's achievement at Glasgow was highly praised. *Dekorative*

THE·DANCE·OF·THE·
WHITE·ROSE

JESSIE·M·KING

37
Jessie M. King, 'The Dance of the White Rose', circa 1902. Pen, ink and watercolour on vellum, 26.7 cm. × 27.9 cm. Glasgow Art Gallery and Museum.

Kunst and *Deutsche Kunst und Dekoration* in Germany, *Art et Décoration* in France and *Arte Italiana Decorativa e Industriale*, all picked out the Scottish section for special mention. *The Studio* was equally enthusiastic and wrote of Jessie M. King's influence on Glasgow book design, suggesting that Scottish art workers could now take their rightful place among the leaders of the decorative art movement in Europe.

In August 1902 Jessie received *The Studio*'s accolade of an extended article on her work. The author, Walter R. Watson, wrote frankly about her limitations as a student and her various failings in her academic work, but he acknowledged her considerable talent and complimented Newbery for fostering it without attempting to force it into unnatural moulds. He remarked on Jessie's preoccupation with the spiritual and symbolic aspects of nature and her attempts to look beyond the outward show to the poetry hidden within. He mentioned the influence of Beardsley and praised the way Jessie handled her chosen themes of Scottish ballads and northern fairy tales. The article was illustrated with several examples of Jessie's work chosen to show her versatility. It reproduced the Rowat bookplate and the binding of *L'Evangile de l'Enfance* as examples of her more formal linear designs. It showed a magnificent drawing she had done for the title page of a proposed

38
Aubrey Beardsley, 'The Dream', 1896. Pen and ink illustration for The Rape of the Lock *by Alexander Pope published by Leonard Smithers.*

39
Jessie M. King, 'At the Gate of the House of Dreams', 1902. Pen and ink on vellum, 22.9 cm. × 19.7 cm. Private collection.

40
Jessie M. King, proposed title page for Fairy Tales *by Hans Anderson, circa 1902. Pen and ink on vellum, 31.1 cm. × 23.5 cm.*

Hans Andersen that was so finely detailed that the illustration seemed to be made up entirely of minute dots that had coalesced here and there to form garlands or dewdrops in a spider's web. It was a triumph of painstaking exactitude and demanded acute eyesight and penmanship of the highest order. Jessie built up many drawings in this way: the Rossetti binding, *The Moon Child*, after a story by Fiona Macleod, *The Dance of the White Rose* and, perhaps most successfully, *At the Gate of the House of Dreams*. They were all related in style to Beardsley's illustrations for *The Rape of the Lock*. Jessie owned a copy of the book and was certainly influenced by the use of dots to make up the embroidery patterns on the fabrics, whilst the very shape of the dresses and the epicene figure she drew in a fan design at the time confirmed her awareness of Beardsley's manner of working. Some of the illustrations in the article showed up Jessie's weaknesses. Her range of facial expression was limited. Some of her compositional devices were unsuccessful, as when arcs clashed against arcs of different radius, and she never learned to draw armour convincingly. She could beguile the eye with heavy decoration but when armour had to be kept plain she left it looking awkward and unnatural. But these lapses were few. The backgrounds to some of her drawings showed an increasing attention to detail in landscape, with walls and roofs patiently built up stone by stone as if she herself were responsible for guaranteeing their stability. The most beautiful drawing of all was *The Little Princess and the Peacock*, and here the rhythmic sweep of the briar about the head of the princess, as it harmonised perfectly with the sensuous curve of the peacock's body, showed her art in all its expressive beauty.

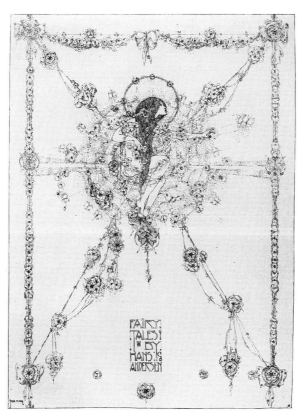

41
Jessie M. King, 'The Moon Child', circa 1901. Pen, ink and watercolour on vellum, 24.1 cm. × 20.9 cm. Private collection.

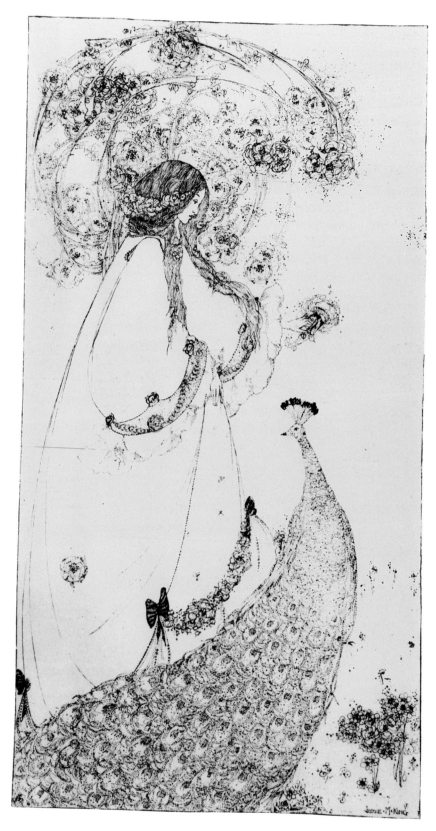

42
Jessie M. King, 'The Little Princess and the Peacock', circa 1902. Pen and ink on vellum.

E. A. Taylor, meanwhile, had been promoted to the position of chief designer in the Art Furniture department at Wylie's and was chosen to design a complete dining room for their pavilion at the Glasgow International Exhibition of 1901. Taylor's patterns, like Mackintosh's, reduced objects to their simplest form. He stained or painted his furniture in plain, often unusual, colours and displayed it in rooms with pale coloured walls and stencilled friezes. His room at the Glasgow exhibition was decorated in light purple and green, which made it stand out from the surrounding exhibits done in traditional dark oak and pine. Lord and Lady Weir, the Duke and Duchess of Fife, who opened the exhibition, were so impressed with the room that they commissioned Taylor to design an identical one for their town house in Glasgow. The accompanying publicity did much to establish him as one of the leaders of modern Scottish interior design. The German scholar, Hermann Muthesius, who was carrying out research at the time for his influential book *Das Englische Haus*, looked upon Taylor as an authority on the new trends in

43 *Jessie M. King and E. A. Taylor, design for memorial window, circa 1919. Pen, ink and watercolour.*

44 *E. A. Taylor, cartoon for stained-glass window, 'Kilmeny', 1902. Watercolour.10.8 cm. × 20.9 cm. Private collection.*

British furniture, consulted him extensively and considered him second only to Mackintosh as a designer.

Taylor's greatest proficiency was in stained-glass design. Around the turn of the century it was fashionable to use panels of stained-glass with scenes of figures in landscapes to decorate doors and windows in private houses. Taylor's glass, like that of his mentor, Oscar Paterson, the leading Scottish stained-glass designer, combined a Japanese feeling for balance and space with an Impressionist attitude in which shadows did not mean a lack of light but a change of colour. Two of Taylor's panels were included in an international exhibition of arts and crafts which *The Studio* promoted in 1902, and both received special mention for their beautiful line and colour. His stained glass was illustrated on several occasions in *The Studio Year Book of Decorative Art* and, until the fashion for domestic stained-glass changed in the 1920s, it was sought after in many parts of the world. After the First World War he designed memorial windows for churches, on one occasion collaborating with Jessie and using one of her designs of knights and angels as the theme of the window. His artistic abilities, his literacy and his knowledge of the art world led to his eventually being made a regular correspondent of *The Studio*, and this brought him appointments as lecturer in design at both the Glasgow School of Art and the Glasgow & West of Scotland Technical College.

Wylie & Lochhead's pavilion at the Glasgow International Exhibition was used again as the centrepiece of an exhibition of British Arts and Crafts held in September 1902 in Budapest where Taylor had the honour of being asked to exhibit alongside the leaders of the Arts and Crafts Movement, Walter Crane and Arthur Gaskin. There was a strong Scottish representation at the exhibition and, in addition to work by Fra Newbery, George Walton and Ann Macbeth, ten of Jessie M. King's drawings were displayed. Jessie was now receiving recognition as the principal decorative illustrator within the Glasgow movement, and her proficiency in this field made it fitting that she was now introduced to the natural outlet for these talents, that of the actual illustration of books.

CHAPTER SIX

Splendours of Pageantry

45
Jessie M. King, 'Yet Misery Holds Me'. Illustration for Jeptha *by George Buchanan 1902. Pen and ink on vellum.*

Jessie's success in Turin, and the publicity she was receiving in the art magazines, encouraged British publishers to take an interest in her work. In 1902 Gardener of Paisley commissioned five illustrations from her for an edition of George Buchanan's *Jephtha*. The scenes she chose to illustrate were the first of many in which courtly figures moved gently through gardens of looped rose bushes, and flocks of birds swept across a sky made up of plaits of wavy strands. The printing of the *Jephtha* illustrations, though, was heavy and insensitive, and the harsh blackness of the lettering at the foot of each one quite destroyed the feeling of serenity that Jessie had wished to convey.

In that same autumn she signed a contract with Routledge to provide three cover designs and no fewer than twenty-four sets of lettering for a series of children's classics, such as *Don Quixote* and *Lamb's Tales from Shakespeare*. The cover designs, which were meant to relate to different age-groups, depicted three stages of maturity in a young girl. The first had a fairy child sitting in a rose briar; the second, a short-skirted girl walking through a flower-covered meadow; and the third, an older girl in a full-length dress standing between rose trees. All three figures were framed by rose stems, and flights of swallows flew past their heads. With those extra touches of sensitivity Jessie also introduced tiny, quite unnecessary, but utterly delightful motifs into the design so that, for example, she made a single swallow fly through a rectangle of briar and a butterfly hover in the air for a fairy to rest its feet on.

J. M. Dent, too, wanted her to illustrate for them. Towards the end of 1902 she drew a frontispiece for their edition of *The Mabinogion*, and this led to a more substantial commission for the decorations and illustrations for a translation of the French romance *The High History of the Holy Graal*. Although it came early in her career, this sumptuously produced book, even more opulent in its de-luxe edition with a vellum binding tooled in gold and blue, and with the illustrations printed on India paper, was one of Jessie's most important achievements. In addition to the decorations for the cover and the preliminaries Jessie designed thirty-six ornamental headpieces and twenty-two full-page illustrations, many with elaborate borders in red and black similar to the ones done by Burne-Jones and William Morris for the Kelmscott Press (see plate 47). Jessie's drawings stressed the fantastic elements in the story. The columns in the halls were ornate with jewels and wreathed in spirals of carved fruit and blossom. Clouds were made up of tumbling balls of minute dots, and the air was filled with stars and petals. The ladies' dresses

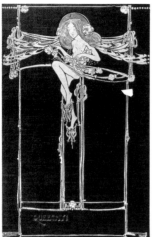

were of fine lawn, totally unsuitable for the cold northern climate of the setting but ideal for the eternal Spring of legend. The illustrations gave the reader a glimpse of a land and time remote from reality, as if the artist had been allowed access to the same ancient truths from which the legends had grown. In some of the drawings Jessie drew a second border inside the main one and linked the two areas with 'corner stops' of decoration, so that the picture appeared to be suspended inside a large mount. This tended to distance the reader from what went on in the scene and helped to emphasise the decorative aspects of the illustrations. Jessie's device of a rectangle within a rectangle was really an elaboration of her grid pattern, and she used it as the structural basis of many of her works in a great variety of ways (see also plates 46, 58, 62, 63, 84, 87, 93).

She spent the summer of 1902 on a sketching tour of Europe. Adah had come over from Berlin for Eva's wedding and had persuaded Jessie to go back

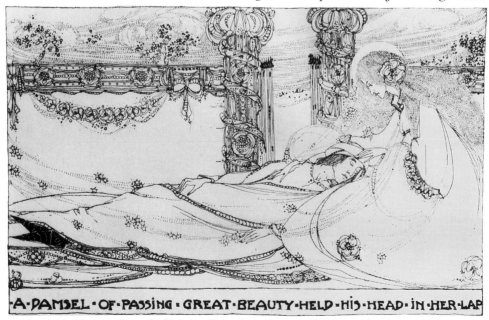

47 *Jessie M. King, 'A Damsel of Passing Great Beauty', 1903. Illustration for* The High History of the Holy Graal. *Pen and ink on vellum.*

48
Jessie M. King,
'Nuremberg', 1902. Pen and
ink on vellum.

46

with her. The spur to action came from an award that Jessie had received of one of the smaller travelling scholarships that the Glasgow School of Art offered each year. She had delayed using it and decided to add part of the modest sum of money that her father had left her and turn the trip into a major tour of European art centres. With Mary as maid and chaperone Jessie went first to Berlin to stay with Adah. They travelled to Dresden to see Raphael's *Sistine Madonna*, and from there went on to Nuremberg. They took trips to the little medieval town of Rothenberg where Jessie, who was sketching and making study notes the whole time, was fascinated by the buildings with their fairy-tale rooftops. She drew the little hillside towns and villages of the region and delighted in the contrast between the rough stone of the walls and the red tiles of the roofs, sometimes adding to the fantasy of a scene by drawing puffballs of cloud rolling down over the buildings. They went over to Italy and stayed in Siena with its liquorice-toffee cathedral, and ended their journey in Florence, where Jessie was able to see in real life the Botticellis in the Uffizi, bigger and much richer in colour than her own reproductions had led her to believe. In all, she and Mary were away a month, and they returned at the end of September in time for the new term.

As soon as she got back Jessie began work for Routledge on a title-page and four illustrations for Charles Kingsley's *The Heroes*. The title-page was another subtle variation on the grid pattern and consisted of a long rectangle with asymmetrical decoration, not unlike Glasgow-Style furniture.

The border was thin and wavering, like Beardsley's dripping candle-wax, with the title at the top and the publisher's name at the bottom. In between was a large area of blank space. Tiny nodules of loops or roses or jewels punctuated the line which would sometimes leave these nodes as double or triple strands, only to revert to a single one at the next stop. The illustrations again pictured knights and ladies in courteous exchanges but, as in the Gardener book, poor printing spoilt Jessie's beautiful work and made the drawings look as if they had been deliberately left blank for colouring in by the reader.

The true subtlety of Jessie's art was seen the following year in a drawing she exhibited at the new Glasgow Society of Artists. She had been elected to the committee under the presidency of John Hassall and had designed the cover for the catalogue of this, their second exhibition. Her entry, *At the Gate of the House of Dreams*, had already been mentioned in *The Studio* and was one of the most beautiful of all Jessie's drawings. It shows a young girl dressed simply in a plain, long-sleeved gown, walking towards the Land of Dreams. Her eyes are open but vacant, as if she were sleepwalking, but her long neck and pointed chin give her an air of expectancy within the remoteness. Thick, shoulder-length hair, drawn as a mass of dots, covers her ears in the Burne-Jones manner and is held in place at the side with a rose. A halo of rose petals surrounds her head and, in her left hand, she carries a single rose as a light or talisman on her journey through her dream. Her right hand is stretched out tentatively, as if she is a little afraid to make contact with the welcoming hand of one of the maidens in the House of Dreams. The young girl approaching the House comes from the real world and so Jessie drew her in unbroken line. The other characters, from the world of dreams, were drawn entirely in dots, like the beginning of Creation when molecules were condensing into substance. Only their hands and feet, which were their points of contact with the outside world, were drawn in outline. The wonder of the drawing lay in its execution. No line obtruded and no harsh mark could be seen. In its own way it celebrated Jessie M. King's attainment of artistic maturity and a confidence in her unique manner of self-expression. It was her own arrival at her House of Dreams.

Routledge continued to offer her work. During the spring and summer of 1903 Jessie illustrated four of their 'Broadway Booklets': square, pocket-sized books with coloured covers of stiff card and four black-and-white illustrations in each one. Three of the volumes: *Elaine*, *Guinevere* and *Morte d'Arthur*, were of excerpts from Tennyson's *Idylls of the King*. The fourth was *The 'Rubáiyát of Omar Khayyám'*—a book every publisher in those days had to have on his list. The King Arthur illustrations were of the castles and spacious halls, inhabited by knights and ladies, that Jessie did so well. She drew fluted columns and pillars like bundles of candlewax and linked them at the top with parallel bands of freely drawn lines to suggest roughly hewn beams. The little boat with the billowing sails that she had first used in the School competition, appeared again, now hung with garlands, and steered on choppy seas, without apparent effort, by the two queens. Jessie was fond of her magic ship and used it in later illustrations for *The Defence of Guinevere*, *The Poems of Spenser*, and in her bookplates and greetings cards.

50
Jessie M. King, 'At the Gate of the House of Dreams', detail. Pen and ink on vellum. 22.9 cm. × 19.7 cm. Private collection.

51
Jessie M. King, design for greetings card, 'Kind Winds', circa 1909. Pen, ink, watercolour, silver and gold on vellum.
21.6 cm. × 12 cm. Private collection.

52
Jessie M. King, 'The Islands of Phaedra and Acrasia' from The Poems of Spenser *1906. Pen and ink and gold on vellum,*
19.7 cm. × 11.4 cm.

53
Jessie M. King, 'Where I made one turn down an empty glass'. Illustration from The Rubaiyat of Omar Khayyam, *1903. Pen and ink on vellum.*

54
Jessie M. King, 'The Flower Fairy in The Magic Garrett', 1903. Illustration from Littledom Castle and other Tales *by Mrs M. H. Spielman, (detail) 1903. Pen and ink.*

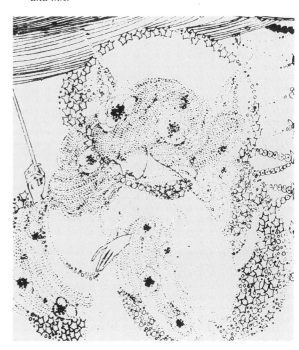

The illustrations in these 'Broadway Booklets' again showed how hard Jessie found it to draw beautiful faces. Wherever possible she avoided front views because the fineness of her line and her avoidance of shading made expression difficult and her stylisation all too evident. Consequently, the unvarying straight foreheads, the sharp noses and the pointed chins, always in profile, gave many of her faces a severity that the gentleness of their eyes was never really able to soften. Hands, though, which most artists cannot draw expressively, gave her no difficulty. All her figures, both male and female, had sensitive hands suitable for healing or blessing, and this gave them the grace that their faces were never quite able to match.

The 'Broadway' drawings contained several Beardsleyan touches. The *Rubáiyát* illustrations, like Beardsley's for *Salome*, contrasted plain white areas with bands of rich pattern. In many of them Jessie used Beardsley's structural method of running a vertical line, usually a rose stem, from the top to the bottom of a picture. All the illustrations included haloes of stars and petals in a variety of forms, flights of stylised swallows, and loops and knots of briar, all drawn in the most delicate penwork. It was 'pen embroidery', a term that one critic used to describe another of her illustrations, 'The Magic Garret', which she did for *Littledom Castle*, a compendium of fairy tales compiled by Mabel Spielmann. In its way, this single drawing attested to the professional recognition of Jessie as one of the great illustrators of the day, for her fellow artists in the book included Kate Greenaway, Arthur Rackham and Hugh Thomson.

In 1903 Jessie also designed a group of exquisite nursery postcards for the Glasgow firm of Miller & Lang. Picture postcard manufacture was a considerable industry around the turn of the century. The best cards, both in printing and design, came from Germany. Miller & Lang attempted to establish a British counterpart in their 'National Series'. They invited Jessie M. King, as the foremost Scottish illustrator, to design a set of six nursery rhymes to be printed in colour on card textured to simulate watered silk. The illustrations for 'The Queen of Hearts', 'All the King's Men', 'Little Miss Muffett', 'Hark, Hark the Dogs do Bark', 'Little Boy Blue' and 'Mary, Mary', were the first Jessie had done entirely in watercolour. Up to that time she had used colour sparingly, enlivening an occasional flower or a bird with a mere suggestion of blue, silver or gold. For the postcards she used stronger colours much more broadly applied. Pinks, greens, yellow and gold enriched what were already completed pen-and-ink drawings, even to the extent of making them appear slightly overdone. She gave the figures a Japanese look with sweeping, kimono-like gowns and, occasionally, as in the figures in 'Hark, Hark', an angularity that was to become one of the characteristics of her later work. The cards were beautiful, possibly the most attractive examples of the period, but, even at the modest price of sixpence for the set, the venture proved uneconomical and Miller & Lang had difficulty in disposing of their stock. There were no repeat commissions and the firm turned to publishing the comic cards that had always been more popular.

That year, Jessie was also invited to design an advertisement card for Kate Cranston's Ingram Street Tea Rooms. By 1903, three of the famous tea rooms had been opened, decorated in the Glasgow Style variously by George

55
Miss Kate Cranston circa 1905. T & R Annan & Son.

50

HARK·HARK·THE·DOGS·DO·BARK·
THE·BEGGARS·ARE·COMING·TO·TOWN·

*56
Jessie M. King, nursery
postcard 'Hark, Hark',
1903. Collection Nial
Devitt.*

Walton, Mackintosh and the Macdonald sisters. Jessie's advertisement card
was done in the manner of the nursery postcards and showed a young lady in
a long-sleeved Japanese gown, posed in a very Aesthetic 'S' shape. On the
back of the card was an announcement in Jessie's distinctive lettering that
Miss Cranston had now installed a telephone service and that 'the company's
charge is one penny per message to be placed in the box beside either
instrument'. Jessie designed three such cards over the years for Miss
Cranston's. The second, in 1906, was more pastoral in style and featured a
slender, dreamy-eyed Marie Antoinette shepherdess with crook and ribboned

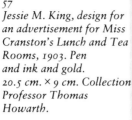

58
Jessie M. King, design for an advertisement for Miss Cranston's Lunch and Tea Rooms, 1913. Hunterian Art Gallery, Glasgow.

57
Jessie M. King, design for an advertisement for Miss Cranston's Lunch and Tea Rooms, 1903. Pen and ink and gold. 20.5 cm. × 9 cm. Collection Professor Thomas Howarth.

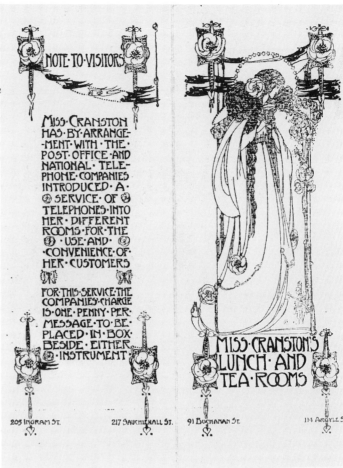

bonnet. The third card, which was the best of the three, was done in 1913 when Jessie was living in Paris. The illustration of girls taking tea on an idyllic summer day carried something of the nostalgia of Georgian poetry, and its beautiful drawing and sensitive balance between the lettering at the head and foot of the card made it one of Jessie's most perfect designs.

In September 1903 Jessie, together with E. A. Taylor, who had recently been appointed Lecturer in Furniture Design at the Glasgow School of Art, and other members of the staff, organised a pageant that Fra Newbery had devised to celebrate the granting by Royal Charter of city arms to Glasgow. The rediscovery in the nineteenth century of the splendours of pageantry was part of the renewed interest in medievalism that had been started in England by the architect Alfred Pugin in his attempts to redefine an English architectural style. His revival of English 'Gothic' reawakened interest in other aspects of medieval history and art. Whatever belonged to the Middle Ages was idealised and looked upon as artistically honest. Hand-crafting was held to be nobler than machine-crafting. The present day, on the other hand, was felt to have been tainted and degraded by industrialisation. This adulation of medievalism spread to the other arts. The search for authenticity in painting, and the interest in legends and literature of bygone days, whether in Chaucer, Dante, Mallory or Shakespeare, was part of a nostalgia

59
Jessie M. King as St Margaret of Scotland, 1906.

60
Jessie M. King, as 'The Angel of the Spirit', blesses E. A. Taylor, as 'Sir Perceval', in 'The Masque of Science and Art', 1905.

61
Jessie M. King costume design for Scottish National Pageant, revised presentation, Glasgow 1908.

for the supposed golden age. Tennyson's epic poetry and the whole of the Pre-Raphaelite movement was an attempt to bring back a world that was being admired for something it never actually contained. The Arts and Crafts Movement arose from this romantic idealism, and its encouragement of pageants was part of its belief in the dignity of labour, the need for renewed fellowship amongst craftsmen and solidarity with the public at large. In 1899 Ashbee's Art Workers Guild—the very name was an acknowledgement of the medieval sympathies of the movement—performed a 'Masque of Winter and Spring' in praise of the newly formed London County Council. Fra Newbery's 'Masque of the City Arms' was originally intended for performance at the School's Annual Dance. The text, in both Latin and English, was a grandiloquent panegyric by Newbery himself. Its very pomposity made it awesome. 'Glasgow! Empire City proud/Flourish thou by Faith endowed/Nor shall Time thy glories shroud/Flourish! Flourish! Glasgow', was the stuff of hymn and Empire, and a sincere expression of the civic and national pride of its day. The list of participants read like a catalogue of the Glasgow movement, and the splendour of the costumes and settings did much to ensure the success of the event. Newbery was asked to mount a more elaborate version for public presentation, and this was produced two years running, in 1905 and 1906, to an equally enthusiastic reception. The *Glasgow Herald*, in a long review, mentioned especially E. A. Taylor, 'in sonorous voice', as St Kentigern, and Jessie M. King, whom they described as an artist who worked 'in fine line reminiscent of Beardsley, but without the sensuous suggestion of that artist' and 'whose weird dress as the Chieftainess of the Twa Corbies was one of the best designed costumes in the Masque'.

It was from Fra Newbery that Jessie M. King and E. A. Taylor acquired their

62 & 63
Jessie M. King, cover illustration for The Life of Saint Mary Magdalene, *1904. Published by J. M. Dent. Cover illustration for* The Defence of Guenevere and other Poems *by William Morris, 1905. Published by J. M. Dent. 14.6 cm. × 11.4 cm.*

enthusiasm for pageantry. In December 1905 Newbery produced a 'Masque of Science and Art' to mark the opening of the Glasgow & West of Scotland Technical College. Jessie played 'The Angel of the Spirit' and Ernest, who had been appointed part-time lecturer there also, again played a saint. Jessie's love of pageantry, her flair for designing both costumes and sets, and her ability to organise people, were evident in the many spectacular events that she and E. A. Taylor produced over the years.

At the beginning of 1904 Jessie received two commissions from John Lane. The lesser one was for a cover design for a *Life of Saint Mary Magdalen*. She showed the Saint standing in an arbour, her head bowed deferentially, wearing a gown with huge dolman sleeves. Her hair was thick and heavy, and the whole effect was Japanese in both dress and bearing. The finished cover in green and gilt was notable both for the beauty of the drawing and the skill of the plate-maker's art, for every fine detail of Jessie's line was reproduced accurately and sensitively in the metal stamping. The second, and more important commission, was for the cover design, page decorations and twenty-four full-page illustrations for William Morris's *The Defence of Guenevere and Other Poems*. Jessie brought Japanese elements again into a number of the illustrations with ladies' gowns generously cut but fitted tightly at the knees and made to sweep the ground in overlapping fan shapes. She still had difficulty drawing armour, and some of her knights looked more like insects in the process of metamorphosis than nobles championing a beautiful lady. The head- and tailpieces, though, were delightful. Some were little heraldic banners hanging as if in a chapel, each with its own picture or device. Others looked like brooches or buckles made out of irregular strands of candle-wax. One showed an angel with a rose, another a decorated boat towed by swallows, and yet another a leaping faun, which seemed to have been a special favourite for Jessie used it in several drawings and as the subject of one of a small number of stained-glass panels she produced. The little devices often appeared as corner stops in Jessie's illustrations and in one delightful instance were used to embellish a greetings card, 'Good Luck', which was later adapted for use as a cover design for an edition of Emerson's poems. They also made ideal jewellery designs, and Jessie used patterns very similar to these vignettes when she began to do work for Liberty's.

Jewellery work was one of the crafts that Fra Newbery had encouraged at the School, and casting, enamelling and swageing were on the curriculum. Margaret Macdonald had produced occasional pieces and Ann Macbeth had specialised in the art. Around the turn of the century Liberty's were commissioning original designs for their silverware, pewterware and jewellery catalogues. In 1905, Jessie, who already had a working relationship with the firm through her fabric designs, submitted some sheets of jewellery designs for their consideration. The majority were floral and were related stylistically to the decorations in *The Defence of Guinevere*, but each one was suited to its intended purpose as a piece of jewellery. A sheet of these designs, some of them finished drawings, others scarcely more than the jotting down of an idea, shows the closeness of relationship between these two aspects of Jessie's art. The running fox in one of the drawings could be intended only for a rectangular brooch, but Jessie cleverly offset the severity of the shape by

64
Jessie M. King, greetings card 'Good Luck to Thee', circa 1906. 13.3 cm. × 7.6 cm. Collection Nial Devitt.

65
Jessie M. King, pendant for Liberty & Co, circa 1907. Enamel on silver. Centre portion 5.1 cm. × 6.3 cm. Private collection.

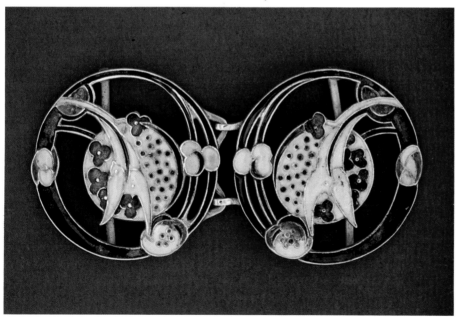

66
Jessie M. King, waist buckle for Liberty & Co, circa 1906. Enamel on silver. Centre portion 5.1 cm. × 6.3 cm. Glasgow Art Gallery and Museum.

68 *Jessie M. King, hairbrushes for Liberty & Co, circa 1906. Silver and enamel. The Fine Art Society.*

making the sides asymmetrical and having it set against a flattened circle. The Yin/Yang curve of the carp in one of the designs, and the heron in another, have a tightness and fitness for purpose that would have done justice to the finest netsuke. The stately galleon was given a setting of suitable grandeur, and even the lesser sketches of lovers' knots and flower heads show Jessie's true feeling for ornament.

Liberty's accepted some of the designs and had samples made up by W. H. Haseler's of Birmingham who were their main silversmiths. The shapes and designs of the book decorations became Art Nouveau jewellery of the subtlest order. Jessie received commissions for necklaces, pendants, brooches, clasps, buckles and even buttons, made up in enamelled silver or gold, with the occasional pearl or semi-precious stone as ornament. Necklaces of gold wire, annealed and twisted into loops and flower heads with a pearl at the centre, became the solid equivalent of the fine line drawings. Fasces of briars were easily translated into wax patterns for casting, and the roses, forget-me-nots and swallows of the drawings became the motifs of the jewellery. They took tangible form as patterns of raised silver and turquoise enamel for a gondola-shaped pendant, or the ornament on the items of a silver dressing-table set, where lovebirds and flowers in blue and green enamel transformed plain surfaces into exquisite objects. Unfortunately, Liberty's designers worked anonymously, and none of Jessie M. King's pieces have her name stamped on the back. The jewellery Jessie designed for Liberty's was in demand for only a relatively short time. After an initial boom, the beautiful entrelacs and asymmetrical curves gradually went out of fashion until, with the outbreak of the First World War, trade in such frivolities diminished and the jewellery commissions from Liberty's came to an end.

Liberty's also sold fabrics designed by Jessie M. King, again, as with the

67
Jessie M. King, jewellery designs for Liberty & Co, circa 1905. Pen and ink on paper. 19.7 cm. × 18.4 cm. Private collection.

jewellery, not acknowledged as being her work. These fabrics seem to have been specially woven for Liberty's by Alexander Morton's of Darvel in Ayrshire between, approximately, 1903 and 1908, and printed by Thomas Wardle's, the textile dyers and printers, of Leek in Staffordshire. Six different patterns have so far been traced, all of them in the style of Jessie's illustrated work of 1902–3, with Glasgow roses, briars, clouds outlined in dots, and arcs of swallows, all printed in pale blues, greens, pinks and lilacs on a white background. The earliest, and only dated sample, 'Rose Trail', is in a Morton's pattern book for 1903 and has an inked inscription 'Jessie King for L and Co.', i.e. Liberty's, together with a note to the effect that she was paid 3 guineas for the design, presumably by Morton's. The same design appears again as a printed linen in a Heal's pattern book of 1908, this time named 'Beauly'. Secondly, a silk brocade designed by Jessie was illustrated in *The Studio Year Book of Decorative Art* for 1907. And lastly, four undated designs, on light silks and cottons, in various colour combinations, are shown in the pattern books of Thomas Wardle's.

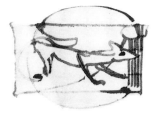

The manner of Jessie M. King's association with Liberty's fabrics is difficult to determine. All three companies—Morton's as manufacturers, Wardle's as printers and Liberty's as retailers—commissioned designs directly from artists. Moreover, both Liberty's and Wardle's imported their own fabrics for printing as well as buying them from Morton's, and Liberty's and Morton's subcontracted their dyeing and printing at that time, usually to Wardle's. A possible solution is that all Jessie's designs of the period were commissioned by Morton's. In 1903, E. A. Taylor was in charge of furniture design at Wylie & Lochhead in Glasgow. Morton's manufactured fabrics and carpets for the firm, and James Morton, the son of the founder and the managing director of the business, was a personal friend of Taylor's and so of Jessie's. Morton eventually made his home in Glasgow and he and his wife visited the Taylors over several years at their homes both in Paris and Kirkcudbright. James Morton could well have commissioned the designs from Jessie (hence the mention of a fee in the Morton pattern book) and, in collaboration with John Llewellyn, the manager of Liberty's silk department, arranged for them to be used exclusively for Liberty's as a dress fabric. Each one will have been withdrawn after one or two seasons and, a few years later, reprinted on a heavier material by Morton's and sold to Heal's as a furnishing fabric.

Jessie's patterns were made up for Liberty's as light dress fabrics which would hang in the soft feminine folds of the Pre-Raphaelite and Aesthetic Movement styles that Liberty's had brought into fashion. By 1909, though, with the arrival in Paris of Diaghilev's Ballets Russes, the pastel colours and gentle designs were superseded by robust patterns in primary colours that had been inspired by the sets and costumes of Bakst and Benois, and Jessie's delicate patterns went out of favour. In later years she did further designs for Liberty's in both printed and Batik dyed fabrics with all-over floral patterns in much brighter colours (see plate 135), and these were marketed with great success in the years after the First World War.

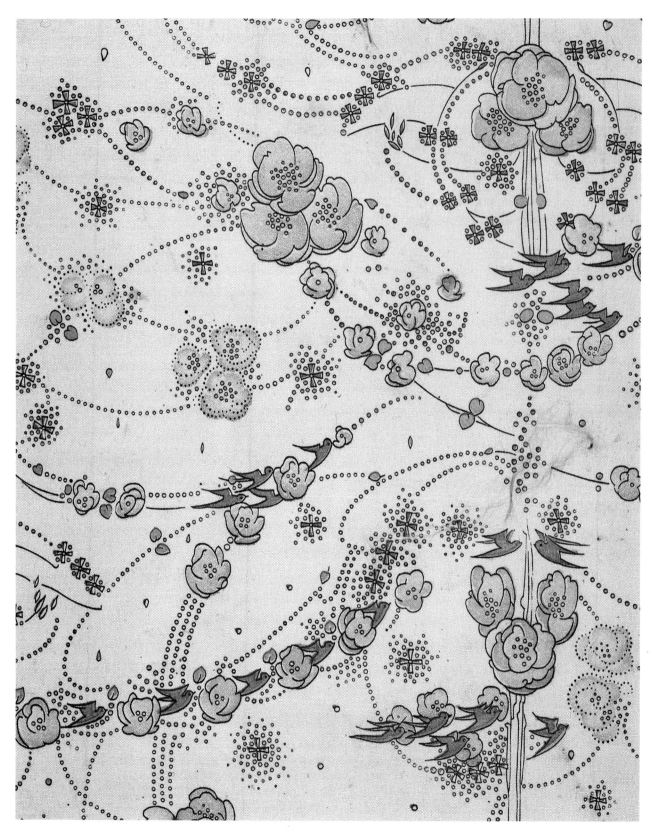

69 *Jessie M. King, printed silk dress fabric, circa 1904. The Whitworth Gallery, Manchester*

· CHAPTER SEVEN ·

Romaunt of the Rose

In March 1905 the Bruton Street Galleries in London mounted Jessie M. King's first solo exhibition. Jessie designed her own poster featuring a knight on horseback, and, although her distinctive lettering seemed rather unconvincing when reproduced on such a large scale, the total effect was arresting and original. The exhibition included more than seventy drawings, most of them in pen and ink on vellum, with some picked out in silver or gold or touches of pale colour. There were designs for bookplates, a fan design and a number of the drawings she had done in Germany and on a holiday the previous year that had included Avigon and nearby Auribeau. The majority of the works on show were illustrations of individual poems and stories that had taken her fancy, and included a sensitive 'Little Boy Blue', a beautifully designed title page and illustrations for Hans Andersen's *The Little Mermaid*, as well as some of the drawings for *The Defence of Guinevere*.

The exhibition showed some of the changes that had taken place in Jessie M. King's style, from the bloodless ghosts of the 'Spook School' days to the more recent sorrowful princesses with their multiple haloes and voluptuous roses. The new drawings, such as 'The White Lady' and 'And she danced to please the Prince' from *The Little Mermaid*, were no longer based on the geometrical classicism of the 'Spook'-inspired style, but were done in a more flamboyant manner which bordered on decorative extravagance.

The landscape drawings in the exhibition were relatively restrained, but each one showed Jessie's individuality. Clouds were like the little puffs of wind that cherubs set in motion in the corners of ancient maps. Trees were almost always thick with blossom or newly in leaf. Tiles and cobblestones, whether in France, Germany or Scotland, always seemed to have been dressed by the same stonemasons. The penwork was always expressive and, in a drawing such as 'Nuremberg', Jessie used the texture of timber or a water surface to create an atmosphere as mysterious as any that surrounded her princesses (see plate 48).

Her method of working was well shown in her preliminary sketches for 'Banbury Cross', one of the drawings in the exhibition. Anna Hotchkiss, a friend and fellow artist, described how Jessie's pencil would dart over the paper, pausing here and there, like a humming bird, to build up part of the picture, and then move swiftly to another corner to balance it. Even before a drawing was finished in its pencilled state Jessie would begin to ink in some of the detail and, if something felt awkward, she would rethink her picture and start again on another sheet. In the first sketch for 'Banbury Cross' Jessie

71
Jessie M. King, 'And she danced to please the Prince', circa 1904. Illustration from The Little Mermaid. *Pen and ink on vellum.*

72
Jessie M. King, 'Little Boy Blue', circa 1903. Pen, ink, watercolour and silver. 16.5 cm. × 10.8 cm. Private collection.

grouped the riders on the left and mounted them on real horses. The crossroads were in the distance on the right. The beautiful harness of the first horse, which contrasted patterned bands against plain white areas, was related both to Beardsley's *Salomé* illustrations and Jessie's own for the *Rubáiyát*, and ultimately became the decorated rockers of the nursery horses in the later versions. Jessie experimented with having just two slender figures facing the lady, but changed this in the final version to a group of four older children. The horses in the third drawing tossed their manes realistically, and Jessie made amends for their being unable to prance freely by decorating their rockers with an arc of love-birds to match the curve of the swallows at the top of the picture.

73
Jessie M. King, 'Banbury Cross' (first version), circa 1903. Pen, ink and pencil on vellum. 13.9 cm. × 12.7 cm.

74
Jessie M. King, 'Banbury Cross', (second version), circa 1903. Pen, ink and pencil on paper. 15.2 cm. × 14.6 cm. Private collection.

75
Jessie M. King, 'She shall make music wherever she goes (Banbury Cross)', circa 1903. Pen and ink on vellum.

Jessie used the 'Ride a Cock-horse' rhyme again that year for a panel of nine hand-painted tiles that *The Studio* had commissioned as one of the illustrations for the first volume of their *Year Book of Decorative Art*. It was Jessie's only venture into tile decoration and represented a transitional medium between her book illustrations and her ceramic work for, in 1906, she was

76
Jessie M. King, 'Sing a Song of Sixpence', circa 1906. Design for wallpaper for Wyllie and Lochhead.

appointed tutor in Ceramic Decoration at the School in addition to her post in the Department of Book Decoration. Her individual approach to nursery themes was also shown in a wallpaper, 'Sing a Song of Sixpence', that she did at the same time for Wylie & Lochhead in which the blackbirds became so many swallows weaving in and out of briars, and the maid at the washing line was transformed into one of her lissom damsels lost in thought.

In October 1905 Jessie signed a contract with Routledge to provide twelve illustrations, at a guinea a drawing, for a new edition of Milton's *Comus*. The drawings were to be printed in sepia on Japanese vellum by the new photogravure process which was capable of picking up every nuance of Jessie's line. Some of the drawings still bore echoes of Beardsley as in, for example, the spirits rising from the cup in 'The Lady Sat in the Enchanted Chair' but, in the illustrations in which Comus himself appeared, Jessie was able to find her own style. She drew him as a gentle shepherd playing his pipe, dressed in a loose short smock, his hat turned up at the back and tipped forwards over his bushy hair, and she gave his eyes the same transfigured look as those of the young visitor to the House of Dreams. She showed an extraordinary range of pen strokes in depicting both the figures and the surrounding scenery, and brought trees and shrubs to life with a great variety of texture and tone. She designed the title page with beautiful variations on her favourite motifs of butterflies, birds and flowers and, almost as an afterthought, she finished off the book with a colophon of a female saint, as if to imply that the concept of virtue with which the poems ends, could be truly fulfilled only in a Christian context.

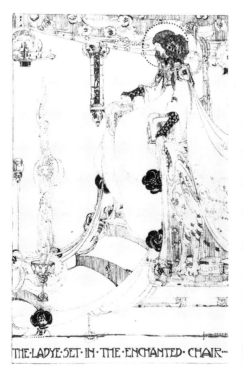

77 Jessie M. King, 'The Ladye sat in the Enchanted chair', and 'Whose Artful strains', 1905. Illustrations from Milton's Comus, *published by Routledge. Pen and ink on vellum.*

Towards the end of the year Jessie joined the Glasgow Society of Lady Artists. This body had been formed in 1882 by a group of former pupils of Robert Greenless, one of Fra Newbery's predecessors at the Glasgow School of Art. Its aim was to provide facilities for women artists who, up to that time, had been forbidden to attend life classes on the grounds of immodesty and unseemliness. Greenless had allowed the Society to hold its first meetings in his studio and, by 1905, the group had acquired its own premises in Blythswood Square. George Walton had designed a gallery for them and they were already planning to have Mackintosh redesign their entrance hall and outside door. The Society was entirely self-supporting and had among its members all the important graduates of the School. It held two or three main exhibitions each year featuring different aspects of fine or applied art, and members were allowed a generous five or six entries. Jessie M. King came to be the Society's longest reigning and most distinguished member, and many of the shows she held there, both alone and jointly with Helen Paxton Brown, were important events in its history. For many years the Society's exhibitions were noteworthy features of the Glasgow art scene but, eventually, lack of support and financial difficulties forced its closure in 1970.

78
Jessie M. King, 'And in the Midst Thereof', 1906. Illustration from The Poems of Spenser. *Pen, ink, pink and gold on vellum.*

At the beginning of 1906 Jessie illustrated two books, *The Poems of Spenser* and *The Poems of Shelley*, for T. C. & A. C. Jack. All sixteen illustrations were sensitively printed on cream art paper with speckles of pink and gold highlighting the black and white drawings. The *Spenser* illustrations did not always show Jessie's work at its best. Figures sometimes seemed awkward and proportions misjudged, as when a horse and its rider were shown in vertical format with half the horse 'offstage' or, in the illustration 'The Islands of Phaedra and Acrasia', where Jessie so attenuated the little ship that the princess steering it appeared to be sitting in a bathtub, and the sinister

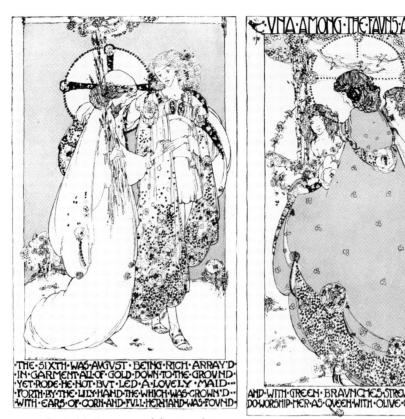

79 *Jessie M. King, 'Mutabilitie', and 'Una Amongst the Fauns and Satyrs', 1906. Illustrations from* The Poems of Spenser, *pen and ink, pink and gold on vellum. 20.3 cm. × 12.7 cm. Private collection.*

overtones of the siren song, that the drawing was meant to illustrate, were lost. However, the beautifully ornamental Arts and Crafts pillar in 'And in the midst thereof', the Botticellian stance of the figure of August in 'Mutabilitie', and the bold sweep of the gown in 'Una among the Fauns', drawn as Beardsley might have done it, were all superb and showed how well she had assimilated some of the styles that had influenced hers. *The Poems of Shelley*, which was published the following year, seemed to encourage a more sympathetic response from her. The line was less harsh than in the *Spenser* book and the actual drawing in, for example, the plain smock of a shepherd set against an almost cloudless sky in 'Alone, desolate and Apart', was simpler and more suited to the poetry. The excesses of the Spenser drawings were toned down and Jessie replaced their frequent brashness with a discreetness reminiscent of the *Comus* illustrations.

1906 also marked the beginning of a long association she had with the Glasgow publishers Gowans & Gray. Several firms were bringing out small inexpensive pocket-sized volumes in card or paper covers. Routledge had their 'Broadway Booklets', Lane their 'Lovers Library' and Blackie their 'Red Letter Poets'. Gowans & Gray entered the market with several series of plays, essays and belles-lettres. Each volume was backed in crisp parchment paper and had a specially designed upper cover. Jessie's initial commission for twelve of the covers so pleased the publishers that it was renewed in an ongoing arrangement that ran for a further twenty-five years, the style

80
Jessie M. King, 'Alone, Desolate and Apart', 1906. Illustration from The Poems of Shelley. *Pen, ink, pink and gold on vellum.*

changing as her other work changed. The first covers—*Our Trees and How to Know Them*, the morality play *Everyman* and Jeremy Taylor's *The Marriage Ring*—were all essentially tinted pen drawings. The small format offered a challenge that Jessie met very well. The cover to *Everyman* was one of the most adventurous, with a kneeling knight set in a small central rectangle. It was a well-thought-out, spacious design and, in the tiny details of the armoured foot projecting into the no-man's land which united the inner and outer portions of the cover, it showed how refined Jessie's decorative sense had become. The contract with Gowans & Gray also included a book of Jessie's own nature drawings entitled 'Budding Life'. Her sketchbooks had always contained studies of trees and plants but, in her finished illustrations, Jessie had always treated natural forms decoratively rather than with botanical accuracy. 'Budding Life', though, recorded exactly what she had seen. The fourteen pen-and-ink drawings were studies of various trees and shrubs at the moment of coming into leaf. Sprays of lilac, chestnut, wild rose and japonica were laid out against the bare whiteness of the page as if the spectator were looking through them into a cloudless sky. Everything was beautifully placed and only when she occasionally rearranged branches in a Japanese asymmetry did Jessie indulge in any fancifulness. There were no flamboyant excesses in the drawing, no stylisation of form and no attempt to reinterpret nature along Glasgow Style lines. And to give a final touch of delight to an already satisfactory book, Jessie drew a beautiful title-page with an illustration of a young girl looking at a bird that had just settled on her hand.

81
Jessie M. King, cover for 'Everyman', 1906. Pen, ink and watercolour on vellum.

82
Jessie M. King, 'Bramble Blossom', 1906. Illustration from Budding Life *published by Gowans and Gray. Pen and ink on vellum.*

The Edinburgh publishers T. N. Foulis also entered the market for pocket-sized gift books. Their 'Envelope Books' were long and narrow and came in a variety of bindings of pictorial paper, cloth and leather, each one with a special wrapper attached to it for sending through the post. The volumes were illustrated with reproductions of paintings by both new and established artists. The Brock brothers, Russell Flint, Katherine Cameron and Maurice Greiffenhagen, who was then Professor of Painting at The Glasgow School of Art, all worked for Foulis at one time or another. Jessie M. King's first commission was to illustrate Keats' *Isabella*. Her six watercolours in delicate shades of lilac and sage green were sensitively done and caught the sense of disbelief behind the grief of the heroine mourning her dead lover. The reproductions, though, were poor, for these were the early days of colour process work, and they hardly did justice to the understanding and sympathy that Jessie had put into her illustrations.

83
Jessie M. King, 'Apple Blossom', 1908. Pen, ink and watercolour. 26 cm. × 36.2 cm. Victoria and Albert Museum.

In February 1907 Jessie held her first solo exhibition in Scotland at T. & R. Annan & Son's Gallery in Glasgow. Annan's were the most important photographers in the city and J. Craig Annan, who ran the firm, was famous for his portraiture. A coloured photograph he took of Jessie, using his own 'Autochrome' process, won an award and was reproduced in a *Studio* Special Number on photography in 1908. The fifty-four works shown in Jessie's exhibition included illustrations from *Budding Life* and the *Spenser* and *Shelley* volumes, landscape drawings of Avignon and Auribeau, and a sparkling watercolour, 'Apple Blossom', that Gowans & Gray had commissioned for reproduction as a framed print. The most beautiful works in the exhibition were the seven illustrations Jessie had so far completed for a proposed *Romaunt of the Rose*. These were fantasies around characters, such

84
Jessie M. King, four illustrations from Romaunt of the Rose, *1906: Clockwise 'The Dream', pen and ink on vellum heightened with colour, 25.4 cm. × 17.1 cm Christies. 'Sorrow', pen and ink on vellum heightened with blue and gold, 24.7 cm × 13.3 cm, The Fine Art Society. 'Mirthe and Gladness', pen and ink on vellum. 'Narcissus', Pencil, pen and ink and gold on vellum, 27 cm × 19 cm, The Fine Art Society.*

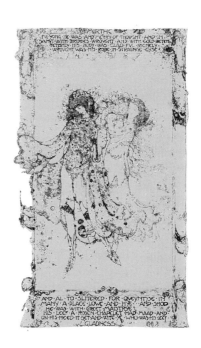

as 'Sorrow', 'Mirthe' and 'Narcissus', in the early part of Chaucer's poem. Jessie evidently wanted the illustrations to accompany a hand-written text for, in addition, she had drawn an illuminated title-page and a single page of text, 'The Dream'. She had written out the opening stanzas of the poem in her block capitals and decorated them with beautiful ornamental letters in blue and gold, and vignettes of angels, cherubs, flowers and birds. The drawings were done in a new, more florid style that she had just developed, and their complexity demanded a technical fluency and attention to detail greater than ever before.

In retrospect, this neo-Rococo style might well be considered the summit of Jessie M. King's art as an illustrator but, possibly because of the sheer intensity of effort it called for, and the eye-strain involved, she worked in this manner for only a very short time. She began each of the new illustrations with a single figure or group, and then proceeded to overlay the image with an ornamental lacing of such intricacy that the subject and form became submerged in an overall pattern. The figures were bound together with bundles of stars or streams of dust particles, so that the picture content became subordinate to the jewelled whole. In the borders of the drawings the small motifs that had enlivened the corners of her noughts-and-crosses grids now began to take on a life of their own. They expanded into panels down the sides or along the horizontals and contained secondary illustrations of angels and attendants, or sometimes actual scenes. The captions, too, which were part of every one of her drawings, grew in length as Jessie used her powerful lettering as a structural unit, so that sometimes the quotation appeared as a large decorative block set inside or outside the pictorial portion, depending on the balance Jessie wished to achieve. The drawings were full of movement. Petals showered down over the figures and there was a wind-blown turbulence that made hair and cloaks and skirts fly out in a delirious waywardness. The drawings were filled with arabesques and cusped forms and sudden changes of direction that exactly recaptured the nervous excitement of Rococo art. The characters appeared to hover in the air with a lightness that matched the dance of the petals. Their flimsy clothes of patterned gauze, with peplums and scalloped edges, freed them from constraint and matched their spirit of exhilaration. There was no background scenery and the figures, drawn with the lightest touch of pen on vellum, seemed to be suspended in a setting of infinite depth. The *Romaunt of the Rose* drawings owed much to Botticelli in style. The joy in the wonder of Creation in 'Mirthe' was the same as in Botticelli's 'Primavera'. The elfin face of 'Gladness' was a Botticelli face, and the very reach of her dainty feet, the flow of her gown and veil and perhaps even the abundance of scattered petals, seemed to have had their origin in that great Renaissance painting or, at least, in Burne-Jones's reinterpretation of the figure, which Jessie had known from the frontispiece to *The Wood Beyond the World*.

Jessie never spoke of how many drawings she envisaged for the whole poem and, of the eight she completed, the last one, 'The Welles', which she showed at a later Annan's exhibition in 1912, only illustrated the 1410th line of some 7500 in the poem. It was announced in 1914 that Foulis were to publish her book, and again, in 1917, that Kegan Paul were interested, but each time, especially with the collapse of the market in luxury books at the onset of the First World War, the idea was abandoned as impractical. Even late in life Jessie had hopes of completing the work. On one occasion she stated that she would publish it herself and have the hand-written illuminated pages of text and their accompanying illustrations printed on parchment in a de-luxe limited edition. In the end, though, the project, which she called her 'posthumous work' was never realised, and what might have been the most beautiful of all her books came to nothing.

The exhibition at Annan's was reviewed with great enthusiasm by both the British and Continental press. The French critic M. P. Verneuil, writing in the magazine *Art et Décoration* praised Jessie M. King as 'one of the most outstanding and interesting personalities of the modern Scottish school'. He wrote of 'the grace of these ornamental calligraphies' and praised what he called the 'suppleness of her motifs and characters and the ingenuity of her composition'. The critic of *The Art Journal* described the drawings for *The Romaunt of the Rose* as 'more expressive of a real possession of a vision in life than anything by her I remember to have seen', and described the images as having 'the hush of sleep'. *The Glasgow Herald* wrote of 'the delicately wrought dream figures' and of the artist's 'remarkable fairy instinct for imaginative design'. *The Studio* spoke highly of Jessie's use of watercolour, and described one of the pictures, 'Yellow Poppies', as being 'decoratively perfect'; the magazine also praised Jessie's drawings of buildings in her scenes of Avignon, suggesting that she showed a natural genius for architectural drawing. The whole tenor of the reviews proclaimed Jessie M. King as an artist who was inspired beyond her contemporaries, and whose fertile imagination revealed wonders that remained hidden from other artists.

Jessie also worked in the style of the *Romaunt of the Rose* drawings for a group of superb watercolours inscribed with greetings of various kinds, some of which were intended for publication as gift cards by the Glasgow firm of Alexander Baird. All the messages were euphuistic. Some, like 'May Fortune's Fairy Barque by Wind and Wave be Wafted Thee' or 'Kind Fates Attend thy Voyaging through all the Coming Years', accompanied designs wishing a traveller a safe journey through life. Others wished the recipient joy, or extended greetings of friendship. Like the Chaucer drawings, each one of the cards seemed to have a special charm as if the delicacy of execution and the sensitivity of feeling that Jessie had lavished on the design had become part of the message. The card 'Merle and Mavis to Sing' was done in pale green with tiny embossed flowers in silver that exactly conveyed the open-eyed innocence that the title suggested. In 'Kind Thoughts like Winged Birds Fly to You' the feeling of movement in the joyous dance was heightened by the petals scattered around, so that one could almost hear the bright ring of the finger cymbals punctuating the rhythm. It was a beautiful series, and Jessie's ability to transform such apparently unyielding material into poetic expression gave her great satisfaction.

In their way the *Romaunt of the Rose* drawings marked the zenith of the *fin-de-siècle* style in illustration for, just as Rococo became the ultimate refinement of the Baroque, taming its aggressiveness to a civilised gallantry, so this neo-Rococo development brought lightness and fluidity to an Arts and

85
Jessie M. King, greetings card 'May Fortune's Faerie Barque', circa 1907. Pen, ink and watercolour heightened with silver. 19.6 cm. × 12 cm.

86
*Jessie M. King, cover
illustrations from
programme of benefit
performance for the victims
of the San Francisco
Earthquake, 1906. Pen and
ink. 25.4 cm. × 19 cm. The
Trustees of The National
Library of Scotland.*

87
*Jessie M. King, 'Kind Fates
Attend thy Voyaging', circa
1909. Pen, ink, watercolour
and gold. 30.5 cm ×
26.0 cm. The Barclay
Lennie Gallery.*

88
*Jessie M. King, Fan design
'La Belle Dame sans Merci',
circa 1908. Pen and ink on
vellum. 13.9 cm. × 46.3 cm.
Private collection.*

Crafts movement that had begun to take itself too seriously. As with all points of arrival, Jessie could choose to return to the style and themes of her earlier work, or to undergo a metamorphosis. Eighteenth-century Rococo changed into Classicism. Jessie hesitated for a while with her exquisite web-spinning and then, discovering both colour and simplification through the work of Léon Bakst and the Ecole de Paris, respectively, she moved into the world of Art Deco.

E. A. Taylor, meanwhile, was becoming increasingly dissatisfied with his working conditions at Wylie & Lochhead, the more so because his standing as a designer had received recognition in an article by J. Taylor, devoted solely to his work, that had appeared in *The Studio* in 1904. Towards the end of 1906 he accepted an offer to become chief designer, specialising in stained glass, at The Crafts, a workshop that his friend and fellow Fabian George Wragge had opened in Salford for the manufacture of high-quality furniture. Wragge offered Taylor a considerable increase in salary and a free hand in the design department. He also agreed to allow Taylor time off to continue his lecturing at Glasgow. With Jessie's encouragement, for she hoped that this way they might be able to get married sooner, Taylor accepted the offer and moved down to Salford. For a year he lived in lodgings at Wittington near the works and travelled up to Glasgow each week by train. At first he kept on the apartment at St Vincent Street but, in December 1907, he sold off his accumulated pictures, closed the studio and removed the remainder of his belongings down to Salford.

Jessie was now receiving so many commissions that she felt unable to do justice to both these and her commitments at the School and so, in the summer of 1907, after fourteen years with Fra Newbery, she left the Glasgow School of Art. Her place in the Department of Book Decoration was taken over by Ann Macbeth, and in the Department of Ceramic Design by Annie French. In addition to the commissions for book illustrations, designs for Liberty's and Alexander Morton's and the exhibition work she had to prepare each year, there were the many ephemeral items she was constantly being asked to do. In April 1906, for a benefit concert in aid of the victims of the San Francisco earthquake, she designed a programme cover with a picture of weeping angels. In 1907 she designed a menu for the new Arcadian Tea Rooms in Glasgow, and the following year a group of some thirty costumes for the Scottish National Pageant of Allegory, Myth and History that was held at Craigmillar Castle, Edinburgh, in June 1908 and repeated in Glasgow in October. The costumes for all 600 participants were designed by the staffs of both Edinburgh College of Art and Glasgow School of Art, and included John Duncan, Phoebe Traquair and DeCourcy Lewthwaite Dewar as well as Jessie herself. Jessie's allotted theme was Arthurian legend and her splendid costumes included a 'Lady of the Lake', a 'Queen Morgan le Fay', and one for E. A. Taylor as 'Sir Perceval'. Jessie's own costume, 'The Holy Graal', consisted of a medieval robe with long sleeves which came down to the palms of her hands, and was patterned with stencilled flowers. Over this she wore a broad satin cloak with large Maltese crosses in appliqué work bordering the edges, and on her head was a simple crown from which a wire halo looped round like some ancient astronomical device. Photographs of her in the costume,

89
Jessie M. King, 'Good Fortune Spin Her Spinning Wheel', circa 190?. Pen, ink, watercolour and gold on vellum. 24.7 cm. × 15.2 cm. The Fine Art Society.

however, show an air of total innocence and spiritual dignity which seem to possess her by the wearing of it.

During her year of freelancing independence Jessie continued to submit work to the annual round of exhibitions. In addition to the regular shows at the Glasgow Institute and the Royal Scottish Academy in Edinburgh, she had a drawing accepted by the Royal Hibernian Society in Dublin, and one, 'The Little Mermaid', bought by the City of Liverpool from their annual exhibition at the Walker Art Gallery. She also had a successful exhibition of her drawings in the unlikely setting of Calcutta where, apparently, every item sold. She designed new book covers for Foulis and for Gowans, and spent part of the summer at Eva's home in Culross making her wedding plans and preparing the drawings for *Dwellings of an Old World Town*, a slim, pocket-sized book that Gowans & Gray were bringing out illustrating old buildings and landmarks in this historic Fife village. She spent a happy month there sketching mullion-windowed cottages in cobbled streets, and tiny sunlit squares of whitewashed houses with corbie-stepped gables, pantiled roofs and unsafe-looking wooden staircases on the outside which led to jetted upper storeys where once hay might have been stored. She gave buildings evocative names such as 'The House with the Evil Eyes' and 'Maggie Rennie's Auld Hoose', and in the evenings she worked up her sketches on vellum in pen and ink and an occasional dab of wash. The result was a pictorial record of an unspoilt, unhurried village, now preserved and maintained by the National Trust for Scotland.

By the spring of 1908 E. A. Taylor had become uneasy at the changes that were taking place at The Crafts. George Wragge had retired, disappointed at the increasing commercialism of his business which, by its growth, had destroyed the intimacy and sense of co-operative endeavour that had been part of his socialist beliefs. Taylor himself was lonely in Salford. He had been appointed to the Committee of the local Fabian Society and elected to the council of the Northern Art Workers Guild. He had a good friend in the painter Charles Oppenheimer, but he found the artistic life dull and his work no longer satisfying. He made the decision he had put off for so long. He found a small brick terrace-house in Bolton Road and, with Jessie's delighted approval, arranged for banns to be put up for their marriage.

CHAPTER EIGHT

Birth of Merle

The wedding took place on 29 September 1908 at Mary McNab's cottage at Campsie. Two of the Revd King's former assistants officiated and Nell Brown was one of the witnesses. Jessie made her own wedding dress of tussore silk and sewed 365 buttons, one for each day of the year, around the edges to weight it down. The Taylors spent their honeymoon on the isle of Arran and, straight afterwards, moved into their new house in Salford which they had christened The Shieling, a Scottish word meaning 'haven' or 'sheltering': a name that they used again later for their atelier in Paris.

Neither of them liked Salford or nearby Manchester. The fastidious Ernest and the newly houseproud Jessie both found the dirt and soot more depressing than in Glasgow. They hoped that one day they might be able to return to Scotland to live in a property, Greengate, in Kirkcudbright on the Solway Firth, that Jessie had bought for £500 in 1908 as an investment. Settling in at Salford was not made any easier by the fact that shortly after their honeymoon Ernest had to undergo an emergency operation for appendicitis and was confined to bed for several weeks. Mary came down from Scotland to help Jessie take care of the house and attend to Ernest's needs and, to everybody's satisfaction, she agreed to stay on as the permanent housekeeper.

With Mary in charge Jessie was now able to travel up to Scotland when she had work to do there. In February 1909 she had a second exhibition at Annan's with some forty of her drawings on show including, as *The Studio* noted in its review, 'a score of dainty watercolours with clever variations on the Japanese-Whistler combination'. The exhibition included some of the illustrations for the *Culross* book, an exquisite example of Jessie's greetings card design, 'Good Fortune', and for the first time a selection of her bookplates. Jessie's beautiful lettering, and her ability to work in fine detail, were ideal for bookplate design. In the course of her career Jessie created some thirty of these miniature works of art for her family, her friends or for private commissions. She worked in whichever style she was using at the time for her book illustrations and charged five guineas for the simpler black and white ones and nine guineas for more ornate specimens with gold or silver. Her earliest bookplate was the one she had done in the style of 'The Four' for William Rowat. The last was done towards the end of her life, in the looser style of her late work, for Liston Selkirk, the son of her former doctor. Most of them, though, were designed between 1902 and 1910. In the early days, when her drawing was tight, the bookplates had a homogeneity that kept

90
Jessie M. King, own bookplate, 'Wilding Things', circa 1908. Pen and ink on vellum.
10.7 cm. × 10 cm.

91
Jessie M. King, bookplate for Andrew Maitland Ramsay, 1908. Pen, ink and wash on vellum.
8.9 cm. × 6.9 cm.

92
Jessie M. King, bookplate for E. A. Taylor. Pen and ink heightened with silver on vellum.
15.5 cm. × 6.9 cm. The Trustees of the National Library of Scotland.

them small and apt for their purpose. Later, when her drawing was much freer, the bookplates became larger and began to look like actual book illustrations with the words 'Ex-Libris' added wherever space permitted so that, as in the bookplate for David MacMyn, the unity was weakened and the design appeared contrived.

Jessie chose the themes with care. Introspective and scholarly people were given a solitary figure strolling in a garden, perhaps holding a book. Those who looked upon themselves as lonely voyagers in some way were given one of her beautiful ships in full sail, often steered by a single melancholy figure. A unique example for Jessie Mitchell included both features. She also did an occasional armorial bookplate, such as the one for Andrew Maitland Ramsay, in which severe classical columns and a black unicorn were twined round with tendrils which owed more to the coquetries of French Art Nouveau than to the Glasgow Style. Jessie's own bookplate, 'Wilding Things', was relatively large, and showed two of her favourite rabbits playing on a tuft of ground by the sea, with an angel in a loose scallop-edged robe acting as a supporter at the side of the drawing. The most beautiful of all her bookplates was the one she did for Ernest. It was taller and narrower than the others and incorporated the word 'Neugealtach', which means 'chivalrous'. The original drawing was more sensitive in line than the reproduction suggested and showed a knight in armour being led by an angel and a sacred fawn with a cross on its head. Bluebirds and showers of silver stars wove about the figures and, in each corner of the design, the little fawn appeared again set inside a black rectangle. As with most of her work, the commissions for bookplates stopped at the outbreak of the First World War.

That summer Jessie, who was now expecting a baby, went up to Edinburgh to make sketches for a new book for Foulis, *The Grey City of the North*. Just as she had done in Culross she explored the back streets and narrow closes of the Old Town. She jotted down notes about the turrets with their French pepperpot roofs, and the mosaic of textures where the old stone walls had been patched with grey plaster, and where timberwork had been incorporated in the oriels and loading bays of old warehouses. Once again she managed to capture the sense of mystery in the narrow streets where old women and young girls, indistinguishable in their black aprons and shawls, stood and watched in silence, carrying within themselves the stuff of legends and past times. Jessie seemed to be able to see dormant life even in inanimate objects. She noticed how a flight of steps twisted and bent as if it were growing out of the surrounding flagstones. Down in Leith she saw irregular little eyes in the walls of the ancient Parliament (or Council) House. She drew Smollett's house in St John Street with its five imposing storeys and its Rapunzel tower at the corner. She went to the Lawnmarket to draw the misshapen old buildings, and drew Peffer Mill House which Walter Scott had used in *Heart of Midlothian*. And, of course, she drew Edinburgh Castle, which looked down over the city like some ever-watchful family retainer. In the twenty-four drawings that resulted from these sketches Jessie showed her understanding of the feel of the place as well as its history, and how she could see beauty in things a less sympathetic eye might overlook.

On 4 August 1909 the Taylors' only child, Merle Elspeth, was born. She was given her first name because of her mop of hair, as black as a blackbird's feathers, and the way she curled up in Jessie's arms like a nestling. Ernest was disappointed at not having had a son but, like Jessie, was charmed by the novelty of a baby in the house. Mary nursed the child as she had nursed Jessie. She looked after Merle when the parents were away, and took over responsibility for her when the Taylors went to live in France the following year. A relationship developed between Mary and Merle as between a kind understanding grandmother and her devoted granddaughter. Merle adored her and was a little in awe of the mixture of folk wisdom and religiosity that Mary embodied. Her devotion to Mary was so deep and long lasting that she ultimately decreed that on her own death her ashes should be scattered over Mary's grave. Twice every Sunday, Mary, dressed in her bombazine best, went hand in hand with little Merle to church. Both Jessie and Ernest were quite liberal in their attitude towards the Sabbath and it was Mary who tried to uphold the traditional Scottish code of Sunday observance. One Sunday, when Jessie had given Merle permission to go to the sea, Mary became angry at this desecration of the Sabbath and demanded that Merle should be allowed to go only when the tide was out and there could be no swimming. 'In Heaven', she declared, 'there will be no sea.' Mary regularly spoke her mind and could be intimidating. Once, when the poet Arthur Corder, a friend of the Taylors and a practising Roman Catholic, asked to be allowed to send Merle a copy of his poem 'A Little Child of Mary', he was forced to withdraw his offer in the face of Jessie's 'But what would Maime say?'

Merle's parents both questioned convention and sometimes ended up with mannerisms and dress that bordered on caricature. As soon as she was old enough to notice, Merle began to resent these eccentricities. Like all children, she wanted her parents to be a shield in front and a support behind. She objected to her mother being dressed so differently from her friends' mothers. When Jessie made Merle wear a fur hat with a 'Davy Crockett' tail hanging down, or when she insisted on Merle dressing up in outlandish clothes for one of her pageants, the child objected violently and became hostile and petulant. The climax in the conflict between Merle and her parents came years later. Merle was clever at school but, although she wanted to go to university to read English, her parents had always expected her to follow their career and go to the Glasgow School of Art. She reluctantly gave in to their wishes but, after only two weeks there, knowing that she had neither the talent nor the will to become an artist, she tidied away her drawing things and walked out.

At the beginning of 1910 E. A. Taylor was invited by a colleague, P. Tudor-Hart, who had opened a private art school in Paris, to join him as Associate Professor. Parisian attitudes towards art and artists were less restricted by social convention than in Britain or the United States. Life classes from the nude did not have the 'sinful' overtones they had elsewhere and there was greater freedom for male and female students to mix together. The abundance of artists in Paris trying to find a way of earning a living had led to the establishment of a number of ateliers where students could receive private tuition. Some of these ateliers, Julian's or Colarossi's for example, had become successful academies which outrivalled the Ecole des Beaux-Arts in the quality of their teaching, and had made their founders wealthy men.

93
Jessie M. King, 'Smollett's House', 1909. Illustration from The Grey City of the North. *Ink on vellum, 22 cm. × 9.5 cm. Hunterian Art Gallery, Glasgow.*

94
Jessie M. King in Paris, circa 1911.

'Professor' Tudor-Hart, as he called himself, had founded his 'Paris School of Drawing and Painting' in the hope of attracting students who preferred the safety of an English-speaking environment within the Paris scene.

The salary, although less than Taylor was receiving at Wragge's, was offset by the promise of a partnership when the school expanded. The proposition was made even more attractive by the fact that Charles Holme, the new editor of *The Studio*, offered to make Taylor the magazine's Paris correspondent. Paris was the centre of the art world, Taylor was unhappy at Wragge's, and he and Jessie were still unsettled in Salford. And so, in April, Taylor went out to see Tudor-Hart's studio in the rue d' Assas in Montmartre and, on receiving assurances about his prospects, accepted the offer. He found accommodation for Jessie and himself in the nearby rue de la Grande Chaumière in an apartment that had once been occupied by the painter Maxwell Armfield and which was next door to the famous Academie Colarossi where Kay Nielsen, amongst others, had once studied. Like so many people embarking on a new venture, Taylor had a euphoric vision of perfect harmony with his colleague. However, petty irritations and unfulfilled promises soured the relationship and the association was short-lived. 'A difficult man', as Mary Sturrock, Fra Newbery's daughter, who had studied at the academy, described Tudor-Hart. Working with him, though, had given Taylor an insight into the running of a private school and, in March 1911, he and Jessie rented a group of small studios in the courtyard of their apartment and opened The Shealing Atelier, a slightly revised spelling of their Salford home, 'Under the Supervision of Professor E. A. Taylor'.

96
Jessie M. King, 'Here's a Rosemary for Remembrance', circa 1904. Bookplate for Jessie Mitchell. Pen and ink on vellum.

CHAPTER NINE

From Paris to Arran

Rue de la Grande Chaumière was a street of five- and six-storey houses built in the mid-nineteenth century. By 1911, like much of Montmartre, it had become a street of artists' studios. Down each side some forty black-painted and blistered doors led to gloomy lobbies with brown-tiled floors. A concièrge's office bulged out on the left side and, next to it, a spiral staircase took the visitor to tiny landings which led to the two or three apartments on each floor. On every half-landing a minute corner sink and a narrow privy were shared by the occupants of the flats above and below. The door of the Taylors' apartment at No. 16 opened into a single all-purpose room—'a silly room', Merle called it—which served as kitchen, dining room, studio and bedroom for Mary and Merle. A door at either end of the room led to the one bedroom, which was so small that Jessie and Ernest had to go through the separate doors to meet on either side of the bed. The downstairs lobby led to a

QUAIS·ET·PONT·NEUF

97
Jessie M. King, 'Quais et Pont Neuf', Paris. Pen and ink on vellum.
17.1 cm. × 22.2 cm.

large courtyard at the back in which an unhappy plane tree struggled with one or two shrubs for life amidst the dust and concrete. On the left of the courtyard a long flight of steep wooden steps brought the visitor to a walkway of rough wooden planks with a long drop to the courtyard on one side and the four studios on the other. The windows overlooking the yard all stretched up to the top of the building and gave a good light for the artists but made the rooms unpleasantly hot in the summer. The view from the balcony was a not very inspiring one of rooftops, less romantic than those in *La Bohème* but sufficient to confirm that living and painting in Paris was the fulfilment of one's dreams. Every morning a goatherd drove his flock down the cobbled streets selling milk. When his customers heard the notes of the high-pitched pipe he blew they let down their pails on string from the upper storeys and the goatherd milked his flock to order. The sound of the pipe fascinated Taylor and, when he and Jessie started their summer school on Arran, he brought one to round up his scattered painting students.

The Taylors advertised for pupils in *The Studio* and received replies from Britain, France and as far away as Brisbane. Some pupils came by recommendation. William Davidson, an architect friend of theirs in Edinburgh and a patron of Mackintosh, sent his young lady students for the Taylors to take under their wing. The Shealing Atelier offered instruction in both the fine and, more exceptionally for Paris, the applied arts, with classes not only in oil and watercolour painting, but also in mural decoration, gesso work and stained-glass technique. It functioned between October and May and left the summer free for other activities. Ernest, with Jessie's assistance, was a thorough and perspicacious teacher, and Jessie's generous hospitality—'those marvellous pancakes', as one pupil reminisced—was an added attraction. Also, working for *The Studio* enabled Ernest to call on many celebrities from the Paris art scene to offer criticisms of his student's work. Jessie and Ernest loved Paris. A friend of theirs, the painter D. A. Richardson, described them as a pair of harmless lunatics who were quite unable to save money. He drew a little cartoon showing them as conjurors making their money vanish, with Jessie dressed in purdah to hide as much of her fair skin as possible from the sun, and Ernest wearing his hair long at the back, both to emphasise his bohemianism and to compensate for his prematurely receding hairline. Ernest's good offices were sought by many artists hoping to have their work promoted by *The Studio*, and he and Jessie became well-known figures at exhibitions. They were friendly with many of the artists and writers who were living in Montmartre at the time. Utrillo, Matisse, Marie Laurencin, Steinlen and Boutet de Monvel, as well as their fellow Scots J. D. Fergusson and S. J. Peploe, were part of their wide circle of friends. They met regularly at Madame Leduc's restaurant in Boulevard Raspail, just round the corner from their atelier, and it was there that they met the young Arthur Ransom who was living in Paris researching for his biography of Oscar Wilde. Ransom introduced them to the poet Gordon Bottomley, who became one of their closest friends and, through him, they got to know Edward Thomas, Middleton Murray, Michael Sadleir. Gordon Craig, Isadora Duncan and her brother Paul, and others of the English-speaking writers and theatre people in Paris. They also made lasting friendships with many of the large group of American artists then living there, including the sculptor Jo Davidson, the young E. McKnight Kauffer, who was later to achieve fame as an illustrator and poster artist, and Frank Zimmerer, who became their favourite pupil and who taught Jessie the art of batik. George Sherringham, later to be renowned for his theatre designs, came to The Shealing for lessons in, surprisingly, woodblock cutting, and the young Harry Clarke, fresh from Dublin on an art scholarship, looked in frequently to discuss stained-glass technique with Ernest.

Jessie M. King had come to Paris with a large commission from Gowans & Gray for eighteen watercolour illustrations for a book by Edmé Arcambeau about the bridges of Paris. Each chapter was devoted to the story of one of the bridges and Jessie was allowed to select any vantage point of the bridge for her illustration. She spent the spring of 1911 working her way along the Seine from the Pont de Tolbiac in the east to the Pont Royal by the Tuileries, drawing both the main bridges that spanned the river and the lesser ones that led to the Île de la Cité. Every day she took her stool, her sketchpads and box of paints down past the bouquinist-lined quays to the quiet of the water's edge where she could enjoy the unusual views of the city that could be seen only from below street level. She used a very subdued palette of pale greens and

A·TENEMENT·OF·OLD·HOUSES·

purples, with a little light ochre for the stonework and a watery blue for the skies. Here and there she put in a figure sitting on the towpath, perhaps a fellow painter or a fisherman or a barge-hand watching the scene. The illustrations she did had an air of peace and stillness, as if they were depicting the canals in the countryside rather than a busy waterway in the middle of a big city. Sometimes she would pause in her work and sketch the barges moving down the river and, in one example, done swiftly in full watercolour, she caught the feel of a misty morning on the Seine with all the evocativeness of an Impressionist painter.

At the same time as doing *The Book of Bridges* Jessie was also working on the illustrations for a little edition of James Hogg's *Kilmeny*, using the same delicate lilacs and greens as for the bridge book to great effect. Back in Scotland for the summer she began work on the drawings for the second Foulis 'City' book, *The City of the West*, which was a pictorial record of old Glasgow. As in the Edinburgh and Culross volumes Jessie did not glamorise what she saw. She emphasised the ruggedness of the buildings and used their granular texture to give character and distinction to every surface. She drew the wooden-fronted houses of the hardware merchants in 'A Close in the Saltmarket' with their timbers hardened and blackened with soot and weathering, like husks protecting their insides from harm. She drew a tenement of old houses near the High Street with little alleyways tunnelling through them to leave them as knobbled and sinister as any of the fairy-tale houses in

Grimm. Only leathern old age, wily and embittered, could emerge from buildings like these; never expectant bounding youth. More than in the other cities she had drawn, Jessie knew every corner and back street and, in her selection of buildings and the way she described them, she seemed to feel it her duty to record for posterity the historical significance of what she saw.

The move to Paris also enabled Jessie to meet Elise Prioleau. Madame Prioleau was the most skilled of the many superb needlewomen then working in Paris. She had seen Jessie M. King's illustrations in *The Studio* and had written to her in 1909 suggesting that they might collaborate on making needlework pictures. They had conducted their affairs by post and Jessie had drawn a small watercolour, 'How the Four Queens found Sir Lancelot in the Wood', for Elise Prioleau to trace on canvas and build up as a needlework picture. The finished work was astonishing in its subtlety and realism. The minute stitches were cleverly angled across the picture like brush strokes, so that the light reflected in different ways on the polished sheen of the silk and gave the scene a three-dimensional appearance. The figures appeared detached from their surroundings, and space and depth were opened up in a way Jessie had never dreamed possible. 'The Four Queens' and a circular panel 'Richard Coeur de Lion' were shown at a large exhibition of contemporary needlework at the Musée Galliera in Paris in 1912. Both works were reproduced in colour in *The Studio* and, in a later issue, the magazine illustrated another panel the two had collaborated on, 'The Approach to the Dark Tower', from Maurice Hewlett's novel *Richard Yea or Nay*. In Paris Jessie and Elise Prioleau worked on a more ambitious undertaking of a group of embroidered panels for a fireplace which showed a forest scene with a maiden for one side and a knight on horseback for the other, linked across the top by a flock of birds flying through birch trees. They also produced a set of Noah's Ark buttons, depicting Noah himself, the Ark and a number of individual animals. The set was included in Jessie's third exhibition at Annan's in 1912 priced at what, in present-day terms, amounted to £30 for each button. There is no record of their having been sold.

The working year at The Shealing, like that of all the Paris academies, ended in late May. During the long weeks of vacation the Taylors received no income and they began to explore the idea of opening a summer school on Arran. The enormous task of transporting and feeding and supervising them there, a party of students from France to an island off the west coast of Scotland, where accommodation was scattered, needed discipline and planning. Arran was already a popular holiday resort and the scenery was beautiful and varied. Many of the local people let their homes to summer visitors and either moved in with friends or went to live in their barns or outhouses. The Taylors did a preliminary survey and chose as a base the tiny settlement of High Corrie on the eastern side of the island, a few minutes' climb from the port of Corrie. Down in the little harbour the smacks and puffers, as the small coal boats were called, were able to come in close to the quayside or the jetty, but the large ferries from Gourock and Ardrossan on the mainland had to anchor offshore. Lightermen would row out to bring the passengers to shore and the local carter would be waiting at the quayside to take them and their luggage to wherever they were staying on the island. The

Taylors canvassed their students and, in the summer of 1911, some seventeen young women were conducted by boat and train from Paris via Glasgow to Brodick on the east coast of the island for a month's tuition in painting. Jessie travelled light with only two pieces of luggage for the whole of the stay. Ernest, who liked to prepare for every contingency, took eleven.

The summer schools were successful and, within a few years, so many students had applied to join that they had to be divided into groups which came out at monthly intervals until September when the ferries ceased

101
Greengate Close, circa
1919. (Note Jessie in black
hat standing behind the
water butt).

102
Jessie M. King, 'Boats in
Corrie Harbour, Arran',
circa 1928. Coloured inks.

103 Jessie M. King, 'Rooftops', Arran, circa 1930. Coloured inks. 22.9 cm. × 28.6 cm.
Private collection.

105
E. A. Hornel (facing right),
E. A. Taylor and Jessie M.
King at an exhibition, circa
1927.

106
Arran, Rooftops 1986.

107
E. A. Taylor, 'The Glen',
circa 1920. Watercolour.
30.5 cm. × 24.1 cm. Private
collection.

104 Jessie M. King, 'The Shed', circa 1935. Coloured inks. 20.9 cm × 27.9 cm. Private collection.

operating. The Taylors needed some meeting place where a group could assemble without overlapping the ones on either side. They began to make use of the cottages in Greengate Close by the side of their house in Kirkcudbright, and they reorganised the school as a two-centre activity. The scenery of the surrounding Galloway countryside lent itself to painting and Kirkcudbright was an attractive estuary town. Artists had already found it congenial to work in and a loosely-knit colony had developed, with E. A. Hornel, whose magnificent eighteenth-century house in the High Street was a landmark, as a central but remote figure. Hornel was particularly fond of the Taylors. It has been said that Jessie had once received an offer of marriage from the great man, and Ernest was one of the few artists Hornel could talk to about literature, and show off his superb collection of Burns editions.

108
Jessie M. King, from a Paris sketchbook, circa 1913. Crayon on paper. 10.8 cm. × 8.9 cm.

DORTE·SAINT·DENIS

109
Jessie M. King, 'Porte St Denis', circa 1914. Pen and ink on vellum. 21.5 cm. × 15.5 cm.

*110
Jessie M. King, 'Haricots
Verts', from a Paris
sketchbook. Crayon on
paper.*

The increase in the number of students, with young people applying from France, Germany, Poland, Holland and the United States as well as Great Britain, forced the Taylors to engage an assistant. A Dutch student of theirs in Paris, L. van Groningen, came to help and they were able to announce in their brochure that classes could be translated into French, German and Dutch. For a fee of seventy-five francs a month a student was offered 'Sketching Classes in oil, watercolour and black and white, with special instruction in composition and the application of their sketches to the making of pictures and the applied arts of Book Illustration, Mural Painting, Interior Decoration, Design and Leaded Glass'. The advertisement went on: 'Ample accommodation can be had at moderate cost at either of the sketching grounds'. The 'ample' accommodation referred to the cottages on Arran or at Greengate. Their appointment was simple, with light from an oil lamp or candle and just cold running water or an outside butt for washing. The cottage which the Taylors themselves used each year as their headquarters on the island was known locally as The Hen Coop, and it became celebrated when, in 1928, Ernest used one of Jessie's coloured drawings of it, under the title of 'The Fairytale House in Real Life', to illustrate an article in *The Studio* on the joys of painting on Arran.

Every morning Taylor blew his goatherd's whistle to summon his students to a preliminary talk on the day's work, and a crocodile of young ladies in hats and sandals wound down the slope carrying carpet bags of sketching materials, bottles of water, refreshments, folding stools and umbrellas, and spread out to draw in the day's chosen area. The Taylors painted alongside their pupils. Ernest worked in both oils and water-colours, painting landscapes in a Cézannesque manner, using colour with great subtlety to structure his forms. Jessie preferred to work on more detailed studies choosing, perhaps, the rocks on a foreshore or rowing boats in the little port, or the end wall of a house. For several years she painted in watercolour with a pencil underdrawing but, in the late 1920s she began to experiment with coloured drawing inks. These offered a greater transparency than ordinary watercolours, they dried more quickly and were easier to carry around. They gave her drawings a greater vibrancy than watercolours from the pan, even to the extent of sometimes bordering on garishness. They also had one unforeseen disadvantage in that some of the colours were fugitive and faded unevenly in strong light. Nevertheless, Jessie M. King's reinterpretation of Arran in these almost Fauvist terms gave the island a tropical splendour far removed from the overcast look given it by other painters.

· CHAPTER TEN ·

Exotic Influences

Gowans & Gray planned to follow *The Book of Bridges* with a companion volume on the churches of Paris. Jessie drew two rather formal illustrations of the Sacré Coeur and St Germain des Prés and then decided to expand the idea to include any buildings in the city she found interesting. She began to go on sketching walks, starting with the district around their own apartment at the back of the Luxembourg Gardens and progressing in ever-widening circles. She filled her sketchbooks with drawings in soft pencil which ranged from characters in the streets and architectural details of rooftops or shop fronts to such monuments as the Opéra, the Panthéon and the splendid Fontaine Carpeaux in the Jardins themselves. She showed how the massive ceremonial arch of the Porte Saint Denis looked in the days when traffic was negligible and the lamp standards on either side were in much less danger of being decapitated by passing lorries than they are now. She also caught the feel of a more private Paris in the tomb of Héloise and Abelard and the staircase of the house in rue Montorgeuil where Mary Stewart once stayed. One can follow her footsteps and pause where she paused to make her sketches, sitting at a table in the Deux Magots opposite St Germain des Prés, where Rimbaud, Verlaine and Mallarmé used to gather, or on a stool in a narrow passage at the side of the Carmelite Chapel near Boulevard Raspail, or in the little Cour de Rohan off Boulevard St Germain where, in a simple mesh of lines, she told all that was necessary about the shutters on a window or the plaster cracking on a chimney stack. She made each scene a personal vision and discarded even finished drawings if she felt dissatisfied with their balance or texture. Altogether she completed around 100 drawings. A few of the more finished ones were reproduced in *Paris Past and Present*, a book which E. A. Taylor edited for *The Studio* in 1915 but, like *The Romaunt of the Rose*, the proposed book on the Paris views became a victim of the war and, although she included many of the drawings in her exhibitions over the years, the series, for the most part, lay in her attic untouched for the rest of her life.

One set of illustrations that did command interest after the war was for a translation of Rudyard Kipling's story *An Enforced Habitation* which Jessie had done in 1914 for publication by Mercure de France. The company closed down during the war but the book eventually appeared under Kieffer's imprint in 1921 in a sumptuous limited edition with the watercolours beautifully reproduced in pochoir. The almost ruthless way in which Jessie simplified some of the illustrations into brightly coloured geometrical shapes was a great departure from her earlier work, whilst in others, such as 'Ah,

III
Jessie M. King, 'Ah mais vous n'avez pas vu l'Angleterre', 1915. Illustration for L'habitation Forcée *by Rudyard Kipling. Pen, ink and watercolour. 12.4 cm. × 9.5 cm.*

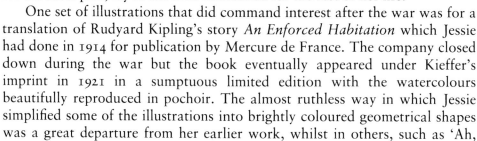

112
Jessie M. King, 'Carmelite Chapel, Rue de Vaugirard', circa 1914. Pen and ink on vellum. 26 cm. × 12.7 cm. Private collection.

113
Carmelite Chapel, Paris. 1896.

CARMELITE·CHAPEL·RUE·DE·VAUGIRARD

114
Cour de Rohan, Paris. 1986.

115
Jessie M. King, 'Cour de Rohan'. Pen and ink on vellum. 23.4 cm. × 15.2 cm. Fine Art Society

116
Jessie M. King, 'Sophie, sa Brosse a Tête en Main'. Illustration from L'habitation Forcee *by Rudyard Kipling. Watercolour.*

117
Jessie M. King, 'The Enchanted Faun', fan design, circa 1913. Pen, ink and watercolour. 18 cm. × 54 cm. Private collection.

mais vous n'avez pas vu l'Angleterre', done in tasteful French pink and grey, with a play of pattern between the tablecloth and the band of horse-chestnut blossom at the side, she graced the original style with a new elegance.

In 1912 one of Jessie's drawings, 'The Lament', was accepted for the Paris Salon and she was elected 'Associée'. In August she held a joint exhibition with her husband at Scheveningen and showed some of the Glasgow and Edinburgh drawings, and watercolours from *The Book of Bridges*. Many of the works were displayed again the following month at her third exhibition at Annan's in Glasgow. The centrepiece of the show was a sequence of six watercolours entitled 'Seven Happy Days', which illustrated poems by John Davidson, and were eventually published in 1914 with additional pen and ink drawings as a Christmas supplement in *The Studio*. Transparent washes of pink, blue and green on the vellum surface made each drawing glow with a soft inner light, converting landscapes into places of secret enchantment. Petals and butterflies in silver and gold fluttered in the air as in the *Romaunt* drawings, and even the faces of the characters took on a serene beauty as they responded to the surrounding scenery. These drawings and two inspired fan designs, 'La Belle Dame Sans Merci' and 'The Enchanted Faun', were among the later expressions of Jessie's Arcadian dream before the harsh realities of wartime brought about a change in her style.

When term started again in October 1912 a young American, Frank Zimmerer, enrolled for a year's tuition in painting. He came to class each day wearing one of several multicoloured shirts he had designed and dyed himself in batik, a process that Jessie had not come across before. Zimmerer, whose shirts earned him the name 'Brother Joseph', after his biblical antecedent, taught Jessie the technique. 'An apple to the teacher,' as she said, and, by so doing, he became the prime cause of the change in her style by revealing to her the dramatic possibilities of colour.

In the original Javanese form of batik, patterns were drawn on calico in hot molten beeswax using small bamboo-mounted metal pipes, *tjantjings*, with stems of different thicknesses curved like the beaks of humming-birds. The cloth was dipped into a vat of dye and hung up to dry. When the wax was

118
Frank Zimmerer (Brother Joseph) circa 1939.

removed by heat the pattern stood out in white against the coloured ground. By repeating the process with fresh wax applied to other areas and using different colours, an intricate multi-coloured design could be built up. The Javanese used mainly vegetable dyes which had a limited, though subtle, colour range. Zimmerer had experimented with the new aniline dyes, which offered a far greater selection of colours, and had obtained exciting new effects. Jessie went even further and applied the wax with brushes to build up pictures on the fabric. She found that she could get a better absorption of the colour and a richer effect if she used silk rather than the customary cotton and, by deliberately cracking the wax before immersing the fabric in the dye, she could reproduce the fine cobweb patterns of her pen and ink drawings.

Jessie found that the best colours were manufactured there in Paris by a firm which supplied them to Diaghilev's Ballets Russes for their costumes and scenery. The Ballets Russes had made a sensational arrival in Paris in 1909, and Léon Bakst, who had designed the sets and costumes for *Firebird*, *Carnaval* and *Scheherazade*, had become as notorious for his discordant use of colour as had Stravinsky for his music. The Taylors had been to see the new ballets at the Chatelet and they had both been excited by Bakst's vigorous décor. Jessie collected reproductions of Bakst's costume drawings and, when Zimmerer showed her how to use these same colours for batik, she realised that they could be adapted for use in her bookwork. At the time she was designing some new wrappers for Foulis. Before 1913, on the cover of, for example, the 'Cities' books or Robert Louis Stevenson's *Memories*, Jessie had used a muted palette of blues and greens. For her new commission of seven wrappers for a series of 'Friendship Booklets', she worked in solid red, yellow, blue and black in a completely fresh way. The strong colours encouraged Jessie to change both the content of her illustrations and the ornamental patterns she was using as decoration. The illustrations for a booklet 'Good King Wenceslas' which *The Studio* published in 1919, and other contemporary

119
Jessie M. King, 'In his Master's steps he trod', 1919. Illustration from Good King Wenceslas. *Pen, ink and watercolour on vellum.*

120
E. A. Taylor, Fashion plate for Christmas number of Gazette Du Bon Ton, *Pochoire, 1916. 16.5 cm. × 13.9 cm.*

121
Jessie M. King, design for 'A Modern Nursery', 1913. From a glass plate.

124
Jessie M. King, 'The Blessed Damozel', circa 1915 cover for D. G. Rossetti. Pen, ink and watercolour. Printed size 17 cm. × 7.8 cm.

THE·BLESSED·DAMOZEL
·BY·
G·D·ROSSETTI

works such as an illustration 'And to the Christening she Came', from *The Sleeping Beauty*, became more spiky than before, resounding with bursts of abstract geometrical pattern and bands of parallel wavy lines like the new hair fashions of 'permanent waves'. What was happening, in fact, was that Jessie's

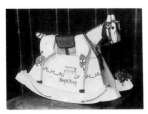

125
Jessie M. King, 'Brightling', Rocking Horse, 1913.

126
Jessie M. King, 'La Vie Parisienne' (second version), circa 1915. Pen, ink and watercolour on vellum. 30.4 cm. × 22.8 cm.

hitherto romantic Art Nouveau style was undergoing a metamorphosis into the strident new Art Deco.

By 1913 the Taylors had become accepted members of the Paris art world. They both exhibited at the Salon and E. A. Taylor had designed fashion plates for the *Gazette du Bon Ton*. In the early spring Jessie was invited to take part in an exhibition of Contemporary Art for the Nursery at the Musée Galliera. A number of French-born and foreign artists living in Paris were allotted space in which to create their own vision of a child's world. Jessie was given a bay some three metres long set against a window, and in it she built up a section of a day nursery. Over the window, to diffuse the light, she fitted trelliswork inset with panes of frosted glass, and a large central panel in stained glass featuring woodpeckers in a birch tree. She painted the same motif on either side of the window and, beneath these, fixed four panels in tempera on wood of scenes from *The Frog Prince*. She painted the remainder of the area white and, along the whole wall, assembled a unit of fitted furniture lacquered in blue and white. In the centre was a settle with cushions decorated with the woodpecker motif set above a line of the little rectangles that the Glasgow Stylists had been so fond of using. Jessie introduced the rectangles again to decorate the floor of the display, as knobs on the cupboards in the fitment, and as pierced decoration on the little Glasgow Style chairs and footstools that she had made. In one corner, on a table, stood a dolls' house in a design that Mackintosh himself would not have been ashamed to acknowledge as his own and, in the other corner, was perhaps the best thing in the exhibition, a modern rocking horse, 'Brightling', that had been made up to Jessie's design. 'One longs to become a child again,' commented the critic of *L'Humanité*, when he saw the display.

127
The Artists of Greengate Close, circa 1925. Left to right; Isabel Hotchkis, Anna Hotchkis, Miles Johnston, ???, Dorothy Sutherland nee Johnston, Dorothy Johnston nee Nisbet, ???, Jessie M. King.

128
Jessie M. King, circa 1920.
(notice the Liberty's scarf
of silk fabric designed by
herself).

When the war broke out the Taylors were in Scotland with the school. They sent the students home and moved into Greengate with Merle and Mary. Everybody felt that the war would be over by Christmas. Ernest, caught up in the patriotic fervour that was pervading the country, volunteered for service, but a medical examination confirmed, as he had already suspected, that the chronic osteitis in his leg debarred him from active duty. In January, with the war at a stalemate, they decided to go back to Paris. Most of their possessions were there, and their livelihood depended on the atelier and what Ernest earned as correspondent of *The Studio*. He wanted to complete *Paris Past and Present* and, if possible, help as an ambulance driver for the French Red Cross. The Taylors found Paris much quieter. Some of their students had volunteered for the American Legion but most of the British and Americans had gone back home. Jessie continued to explore the city for interesting material for her book, and began work on a large commission from Methuen for sixteen watercolours and many other decorations for Oscar Wilde's book of fairy tales *A House of Pomegranates*. She kept the illustrations simple and used pure flat colour to bring them to life, so that, in many instances, the result was like a collage of cut-out shapes. In 'I have never seen anyone so pale', the heroine, looking both classically Japanese and thoroughly modern, formed a distinctive oval that related to the rectangular door and the square wall behind. The three harmonising shades of beige that Jessie used in the picture were balanced by the splashes of orange in the rug and the red in the tiles. With this combination of Fauvist colour and Cézannesque form, even more than in the related 'Sophie' illustration from the Kipling book, Jessie completely reversed her attitude towards picture making. She now built up her illustrations by analysis rather than by synthesis and, even though she still turned to the fairy world for her themes, she made the search for simplicity and structural balance determine the pattern of her work.

By the summer of 1915 the Taylors had come to realise that it was pointless for them to stay on in Paris. As *The Studio* reported: 'The war has resulted in a complete cessation of artistic activity in France.' Ernest had completed the text of his book and had organised the illustrations. Fresh trouble with his leg had curtailed his activities as an ambulance driver, and so Jessie packed what moveable possessions they could manage and, by the end of August, they were back in Kirkcudbright in what was to be their home for the rest of their lives.

129
Jessie M. King, 'I have never seen anyone so pale', 1915. Illustration for A House of Pomegranates *by Oscar Wilde. Pen, ink and watercolour.*

CHAPTER ELEVEN

Return to Greengate

Greengate was built in 1795 by William McWhinnie, a retired merchant from Leghorn, and the cottages in the Close, which ran down the side of the house, were intended as dwellings for his servants. When Jessie bought the property, the cottages were occupied by families of foster children from Glasgow slums. The floors were of beaten earth, as they had been when the Close was first built, and the fabric was dilapidated. Jessie restored the cottages, hoping to let them out to artists, and converted the barn opposite into a large studio apartment. At the bottom of the Close, where the cottages ended, McWhinnie had laid out an Italian garden which ran down to a little burn at the end of the property. This was now neglected and Jessie reorganised it with arches of roses and a vegetable garden at the side which she hoped would supply the family with all its needs.

Over the years many artists came to rent the cottages. Isabel Hotchkiss, the painter, and Agnes Harvey and Mary Thew, both of whom did metalwork and jewellery, Jessie's painter cousin Dorothy Rae and Adah King, on her occasional visits to the country, all lived there at one time. Much later, Merle Taylor made one of them her home. Robert Burns, the head of painting at Edinburgh College of Art, once said that no student could consider his training complete until he had lived and worked with the Taylors at Greengate. One of his students, Anna Hotchkiss, the older sister of Isabel, took his advice and came to study landscape painting with E. A. Taylor. She rented the newly-converted barn and stayed on there for almost seventy years until her death in 1984 at the age of ninety-eight.

The original green gate had been part of a fence protecting the front of the house. When the Taylors moved in they put in a new door at the top of the Close with little Glasgow Style squares cut out of the top as decoration. In an attempt to brighten up the property and perhaps set an example in otherwise dour Kirkcudbright, Jessie painted all the woodwork of the house and the Close emerald green. The name followed automatically. In time, running water was installed to replace the butts and the outside cold taps, but the chequered door at the entrance to the Close and its cobbled path remain unchanged to the present day.

Jessie hung Japanese prints round the walls of the entrance hall of the house and, on the table near the door, she kept one of her hats. If a caller came at an inopportune time Jessie would put on her hat before going to the door. A friend would be greeted with, 'Oh, how nice, I've just come in and haven't had time to take my hat off.' To an unwelcome visitor, Jessie was 'just

130
Jessie and Merle in Kilmeny, Kirkcudbright, 1917.

131
Ernest, Merle and Jessie, 1918.

95

Jessie M. King, 'The Little White Town of Never Weary', 1917. Cardboard model.

going out'. From the hall four flights of steps, 'eight-turn-eight-turn-eight-turn-eight-turn', as Merle sang as a child, led up to the four attics. One was used as a spare room, one was a retreat with books in it, a third was a bathroom, and the main one became Ernest's studio. He smoked incessantly and the room had a permanent smell of stale tobacco. The charm and air of casual confidence that made Ernest amusing company was shed in private when the constant irritation from his leg often made him short-tempered. He worried about his health to a degree bordering on hypochondria. At one time his doctor wrote to him in well-meaning but severe terms to say that his troubles were all in the mind. 'Why', he asked, 'will you persist in chasing the phantom of disease? There is nothing bad. There is nothing at all . . . except in the vivid brain of one who is endowed/blessed/cursed with the artistic temperament.' And he concluded: 'With kindest regards to your Hamlety melancholy self.' Ernest was also nervous of insects. 'Jessie! Spider!', he would call, and Jessie, who worshipped him, would drop everything and run upstairs to evict the intruder. Ernest was dependent on Jessie for the management of his world and, consequently, made her the scapegoat for his short-temperedness. He was precise and meticulous in his ways while Jessie was somewhat improvisatory. Jessie lost things. Ernest never lost anything. Every letter or cutting he acquired was carefully filed away. Typically, he was a good correspondent and would go to great lengths to help people. Jessie, despite every good intention, left letters unanswered and bills unpaid. Her mind was not very attuned to practical matters. In the kitchen she sometimes came up with an artistic 'special' of, perhaps, a large pie decorated with a frieze of pastry rabbits, but it was Mary who looked after the cooking and ran the home.

In the early days at Greengate Jessie did her drawing in the dining room or the attic, as the mood took her. She needed very little space and worked flat, either on her drawing board or at the table. She had a folder of vellum sheets, a supply of fine Gillot metal nibs, and quill pens that she cut herself from goose feathers. She ground her own ink from blocks and used a bullock's tooth to burnish her vellum before starting to draw. In time, when she began to do batik work seriously, she rented an upstairs room nearby and turned it into a studio. Ernest, too, came to need more space to work in and store his canvases, and he rented a former studio of Hornel's along the High Street. The concept of an 'office' fitted in with his structured mind and it pleased him better to go out to his place of work than merely to go upstairs.

Jessie and Ernest had many friends in Kirkcudbright. The artists in the Close and the students who came in the summer added to the vigour and cheerfulness of the atmosphere at Greengate. The Taylors became a link between the rather reserved artistic community and the townspeople, who tended to look upon their artists as harmless oddities. Ernest tended to avoid bonhomie with people who did not interest him, but he was generous with his time for any cultural activity. Drama groups and literary societies from places as far away as Glasgow sought him for his lectures on art, his recitals of poetry and his talents as an actor although, in this respect, Jessie was once heard to remark, 'Don't ask him again. If you only knew what we have to put up with when he's rehearsing.' Ernest had the easy confidence of those born with good looks, and he dressed accordingly in a bohemian costume of a black Inverness cloak with a red lining and a soft hat suggestive of the Latin Quarter. Like Jessie he knew how to ingratiate himself when necessary—a friend observed that they both 'could charm the birds off the trees'—but Jessie's natural warmth eluded him and, over the years, he built up a reputation among the local people for coldness and aloofness.

Jessie, on the other hand, knew everybody. She was looked upon as one of the local eccentrics even though she always denied trying to live up to the image of the typical fairy godmother. However, her unusual clothes and her battered bicycle, which she more often pushed than rode, all belied her disclaimer and brought knowing looks and nods of humouring indulgence from passers-by. She adored children and, when they found that this menacing figure was really one of them, they allowed her to organise them into taking part in her fêtes and pageants. At Easter the children brought their hard-boiled eggs for her to decorate and, where a family was too poor to squander eggs in this way, Jessie would provide the eggs as well. In later life she held painting classes for the 'bad boys' who had been kept back on Saturday mornings in school detention, deciding, with their headmaster, that it was better to channel their energies into something more useful and lasting. She also collected tramps. It was not unusual for her to bring in some vagrant from the street, wash his feet and give him socks and clothes belonging to Ernest. On one occasion 'Orange Meg', a local character, came begging for clothes. Mary was busy ironing her own skirt at the time and was standing in her petticoat. Jessie took the skirt, gave it to Meg and said to the outraged Mary, 'Never mind, dear, you shall have one of mine.'

The Taylors continued to hold their summer school from Kirkcudbright, but the war had blocked their main source of income and they both tried to find alternative ways of earning money. The exhibition at the Musée Galliera had shown Jessie that it was possible to design modern toys that were both attractive and inexpensive to make. She took the idea further by designing plans for toys which could be made out of the simplest material of all, cardboard. She approached the publishers, Harrap, with an idea of a book on the subject and spent the winter of 1916 working on it. *The Little Town of Never Weary* used the framework of a modern fairy story to explain, in line drawings and photographs, how all the buildings of a country town—church, castle, windmill and cottages—might be made out of cardboard. In the story a little girl, Miriam, has a 'waking dream' in which a mysterious White Lady leads her to the magic town of Never Weary and shows her the buildings that make up the story. Jessie drew the plans, made up the models, each one based on an actual building in Kirkcudbright, and had them photographed. She prepared sets of instructions and refined them until Merle, who was then seven, could make every building herself. Jessie dedicated the book to Merle and Mary jointly, but she really intended it as an expression of thanks to Kirkcudbright itself for giving her shelter. In a copy she presented to Hornel she wrote a long inscription in her block capitals, with the now customary dot between each word. 'I think it was a very happy wind,' she wrote, 'which blew me into Kirkcudbright some eleven years ago, and a happier chance which elected to show us a dwelling where one might rest in this spot of the

133
Jessie M. King, 'The Little Mermaid', circa 1918. Pen, ink and watercolour on vellum.

lowlands. During seven years I and mine have only rested there for a little while, like birds of passage making a halt on their flight south. But since 1915 the fates seem to have decided that we should stay here for a longer time, and it was during this enforced stay that the charm of this quaint old-world town took real hold of me, wrapping its mystic web more closely round and going far to inspire the making of my Little White Town. I have but inadequately caught the glamour and allure of its gables and whitewashed alleys—its mellowing chimneys huddled together as if in sympathetic communion with the stars—but my gratitude is to it and its fair welcome and to those who have made its welcome so human, of whom not the least are the inmates of Broughton House—E. A. Hornel and his sister.'

Sales of their pictures, too, had dropped. The annual exhibitions at the Glasgow Institute and the Royal Scottish Academy in Edinburgh continued throughout the war, but there was little demand for new paintings. With an eye to the future Jessie began to illustrate stories by Hans Andersen and built up a set of watercolours for *The Little Mermaid*. She also managed to renew her contract with Liberty's and made a number of floral designs, tighter and more brightly coloured than her earlier ones, for their printed fabrics, with patterns based on massed king cups, roses and gowans. Ernest, meanwhile,

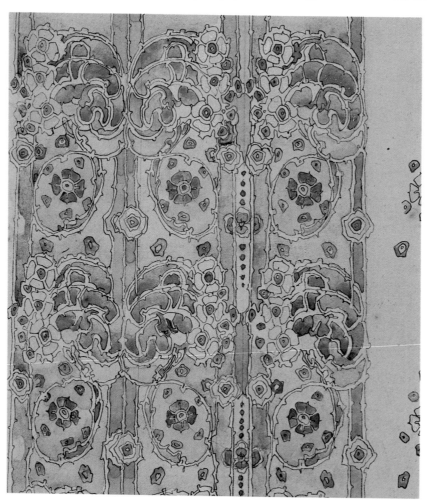

gave lectures and poetry recitals, some of which brought in a modest fee. Both he and Jessie worked hard to raise money for war charities. In January 1917 they presented an evening of tableaux vivants. They selected suitable stories, songs and ballads, such as Burns's 'My Love is like a Red Red Rose', and Keats' 'La Belle Dame sans Merci', for which Ernest recited the poetry and sang the songs whilst the living pictures were being displayed. Jessie, as well as designing the costumes and settings, appeared in her favourite roles of St Margaret of Scotland and Bonnie Kilmeny who was spirited away to an enchanted land. Kilmeny was a character with whom Jessie felt she had affinities. She had already illustrated James Hogg's poem for Foulis and had done a single drawing, in her expressive neo-rococo style, of Kilmeny asleep.

IN THAT GREEN WENE
KILMENY LAY HER BOSOM HAPPED WI THE FLOWERETS GAY

136
Jessie M. King, illustration for Kilmeny *by James Hogg, circa 1909. Pen, ink and watercolour on vellum. 24.1 cm. × 33 cm.*

137
Jessie M. King, 'Little Brother and Faire Sister', silk fabric decorated in Batik, circa 1923. The Stewarteries Museum, Kircudbright.

138
Jessie M. King in The Batik Studio 1934. N.B. The piece on the left of the washing line was ultimately presented to Anna Hotchkis.

139
Jessie M. King, 'The Fairies'
Removal', 1920. Illustration
from Whose Land *published by The Traffic*
Advertising Agency,
London. Pen and ink.
19.6 cm. × 11.4 cm.

Shortly after appearing in the tableau Jessie and Merle dressed up in costume to have a series of photographs taken in the Close and in the fields nearby illustrating the whole of the poem. The photographer was the poet Arthur Corder, a close friend who was known to the family as 'The Man O'Faerie' and who, like Jessie, seemed responsive to the spirit world. Corder, who looked like a pixie himself, was a gentle, self-effacing man who saw no conflict between his strong Catholicism and his belief in fairies. He came to stay with the Taylors on several occasions and photographed Jessie dressed as Joan of Arc, Ludmilla of the Swans and other fairy-tale characters. His death in 1920 was a blow to them all and when, in 1934, Jessie illustrated a new edition of his book *Our Lady's Garland*, she did so with the love and respect of one who had lost a beloved brother.

A second display of 'Living Pictures' followed in January 1918 and, in November, to celebrate the Armistice, the Taylors organised a large Victory Pageant in which Jessie again appeared as St Margaret of Scotland and Ernest as St Mungo.

At the end of the war Jessie and Ernest were undecided whether to return to Paris or to stay on in Kirkcudbright. Ernest was still nominally the Paris correspondent of *The Studio* and they had kept on the atelier in the hope of taking up their life there again. On the other hand, they had been wooed by the charm of Kirkcudbright and the Galloway coast. There was a wealth of landscape to paint, convivial company and a language in which they felt at ease, even if the life there seemed parochial compared with Paris. Also the news from France was not good. They were deeply upset to learn that one of their American pupils had been killed in action. Some of Ernest's finest stained-glasswork had been lost when the château of the inventor Lazar Weiller had been destroyed in the fighting, and a group of Jessie's drawings was missing in, oddly enough, Kiev where they had possibly formed part of the exhibition of modern architecture and design, originally presented by Diaghilev in Moscow in 1913, which had included work by the Glasgow school. These reports, and the stories of the devastation caused by the war, made them doubt whether there could ever be a return to the days when artists came from all over the world to study in Paris.

Jessie, meanwhile, had started to work in her new studio, a single room, some twenty feet square, perched on the roof of a building near the harbour. It was a sensible move for it would have been difficult to do batik work at Greengate. The pot of bubbling beeswax and the smell of petrol, which was used as a solvent for the wax, were a nuisance, and there was insufficient space to stretch and dry the lengths of fabric in the house. Furthermore, the smell of the wax attracted bees and this would have created an impossible situation with Ernest. The new studio added to Jessie's reputation as an eccentric. She found it convenient to keep the colours she ground in old chamber pots. When a visitor climbed the steps up to the studio and his eyes came level with the floor, the first things he saw were these flowered containers with mixing sticks and brushes, dyed cerulean blue, emerald green, fuchsia and deep purple, protruding from them. Somebody, maybe Jessie herself, dubbed the room 'Poland' and the name stuck. 'A tidy shambles', as a friend put it.

In the summer of 1919 Frank Zimmerer came over again from the United States bringing with him stocks of canvas, paper and colours in case there was any difficulty in obtaining artists' materials in Britain after the war. As a welcoming present Jessie made him a batik shirt decorated with Noah's Ark and the animals. With the expert Zimmerer at her side Jessie began to experiment with batik on a larger scale. She had already produced small articles such as scarves, lampshade covers and table mats, and now began to treat larger pieces of silk for use as dress lengths or curtaining, or as decorated panels to be framed and hung. She sent samples of her work to Liberty's and was rewarded with an initial order for twenty yards of decorated silk. Most of her fabrics had patterns of stylised flowers on a coloured ground, but one especially beautiful length, done in orange, fuchsia and purple, illustrated a scene from the Grimms' *Little Sister and Faire Brother*, with a prince and princess and several animals running along a flower-strewn path in a forest. By 1921 she was able to show her complete mastery of the medium in an even more elaborate panel, 'Queen Guinevere Goes A-Maying', in which a crowd of knights and ladies surround the Queen in her progress. Local people began to buy her work. She designed batik collars, and kaftan-like tunics and dresses which reproduced the fine decoration she used to draw on the gowns of her moon maidens. She made batik neckties for Ernest and enlivened her own plain blouses and dresses with inset batik sleeves. A photograph taken in the studio in 1934 shows Jessie at the age of sixty standing by her work table, a small cylindrical stove with its pan of wax on one side and her pots of colour close by. She is dressed in a smock with a batik scarf tied loosely round her neck. A piece of fabric is stretched over a frame in front of her and, above her head, finished lengths of patterned fabric are strung across the room on a clothesline.

When Zimmerer returned to the United States in the autumn he took back some examples of Jessie's work to include in an exhibition of batik he was organising in Indianapolis the following spring. He did much to promote Jessie's work in the United States. He had already arranged an exhibition of some fifty of her drawings and watercolours at the Braus Gallery in New York, and he persuaded the Heron Art Institute at Indianapolis University to take the exhibition, which included some new watercolour illustrations for *Aucassin and Nicolette* and a number of the coloured landscape drawings. Zimmerer adored the Taylors. In a letter to them in the 1930s he wrote: 'My fondest memories are of the days in Paris in 1912–13 and the days in Scotland in 1919 when you helped me, more than words can express, to form my art into a real form.' Earlier he had written: 'I am thinking of all your good criticism and am striving to work in the way you would have me go. I wish I could put into words just how wonderful my year in Paris was, how fortunate I was in finding you, and how much I got from you both.' And he signed himself with their family name for him, 'Bro. Joseph'.

Batik came into fashion. Liberty's bought Jessie's scarves, ties and fabric lengths, and other designers began to work in the medium. In 1921 Jessie gave lectures on the subject, explaining her methods and how she had improved on the traditional Javanese process. The Taylors introduced a course in batik and one on pottery decoration into their summer classes and reorganised the

140
Jessie M. King, 'Saturday's Child', circa 1918. Pen and ink on vellum. 12.7 cm. × 10.1 cm. Private collection.

141
Jessie M. King, 'One day Bimbo saw a young girl at a Spring', circa 1918. Pen, ink and watercolour on vellum. 27.9 cm. × 19 cm. Private collection.

school into two separate sections of an applied arts course at Kirkcudbright during August and the usual sketching course on Arran in September. *The Studio* reproduced the batik of Guinevere in 1922 and 'Little Sister and Faire Brother' in their *Year Book* in 1924. That same year Jessie wrote a book *How Cinderella was Able to Go to the Ball*, which, like *Never Weary*, again used a fairy tale to give, as Foulis worded it, 'practical instruction concerning the new and almost rampageous interest in the art of batik'. In Jessie's version of the story the fairy godmother revealed to Cinderella the secret of how to transform her shabby old dress into the most beautiful ball gown by using the magic of batik. The book was illustrated with tipped-in plates of scenes from the story and diagrams showing how any old white silk house-dress could be converted into fairy-tale material. The illustrations were drawn in a segmented manner that was almost a caricature of the batik process. They showed Jessie trying to reduce her drawing to a cartoon-like shorthand in order to find the essence of the subject. It was as if she were trying to say, 'This symbol represents a pot' or, 'This figure is a Cinderella.' The unsubtle lines and the primary colours were an ideal way of conveying her message to children. The book received lavish praise in the women's and children's pages of several newspapers but, as with all fashions, the novelty of batik faded and, by the late 1920s, the demand for her work had ceased. Jessie continued to produce occasional pieces and, even as late as 1939, at an exhibition of the Glasgow Society of Lady Artists, she showed a new length of tussore, *Morgiana*, decorated with the Forty Thieves, and some scarves with stylised fish and water-lilies inspired, she said, by a day's fishing with Ernest but, by then, batik was no longer making any significant contribution to their income.

At the end of the First World War Jessie began to receive commissions again for book illustrations. In July 1919 she was offered the large fee of £60 by the London Underground, or, as it was then called, The Underground Electric Railway & The London General Omnibus Co. Ltd, to illustrate an advertising booklet, *Whose Land?* telling the story of the fairies who had once lived where London now stands. The drawings were done in a mixture of both the earlier and later styles. The textured bricks and the camouflaged pattern on the birch trees belonged to Jessie's pre-war work. Alongside this was the new shorthand version of flowers and blossom with higgledy-piggledy houses of impossible perspective and fairy figures simplified to such an extent that only a child or another artist could appreciate the concentration of information they contained.

Whose Land? marked the beginning of a new style in Jessie M. King's fairy drawings. Kilmeny and Fand never recovered from the realities of the war. They and the chivalrous knights and ladies, the custodians of courtly love, vanished and, in their place, appeared a new children's version of fairyland. Jessie's drawings had always illustrated stories relating to childhood, but their language was that of poets and lovers. The fairies who came after the war were more earthbound. They had short skirts and bobbed hair and wore skullcaps of foxgloves and harebells. Their land was different from the one that Kilmeny had visited and was more related to the garden at the bottom of Greengate Close, Kirkcudbright. The earlier creatures claimed continuity with eternal things. Their shapes were open-ended and were best depicted in

CINDERELLA·DANCED·FOR·JOY·
IN·HER·SAFFRON-TINTED·FROCK·

142
Jessie M. King, 'Cinderella Danced for Joy', 1924. Illustration for How Cinderella was able to go to the Ball. *Pen and coloured inks.*

Glasgow Style line drawings. The new creatures were much more tied to the real world. They occupied strictly defined areas and were enclosed by boundaries that needed colour to make them complete. The old black and white drawings were a stimulus to the imagination. They allowed the spectator to complete his or her own mental picture from the suggestions they made. The flat colours that Jessie was using for the new drawings made specific statements and presented the spectator with a decorated pattern instead of a window through which he might gaze into a land of wish-fulfilment. For those who remembered the magic land there was a sense of loss and a feeling of resentment. Jessie's new fairyland was closer to reality and its inhabitants looked and behaved like real children. Dreams gave way to simple direct pictorial narrative. The early illustrations had depicted, for the most part, a static world where time had stood still. The characters were largely motionless, dressed in cumbersome gowns and suits of armour that did not encourage action. The new drawings recognised the fact that the world was moving more quickly. The new children were jolly, something that was rarely apparent in the earlier drawings. Clothes were modern and related more to what Jessie saw in Merle than in the visions of her own dream world. Statements had to be exact, lines unambiguous and colours sharp. There was no time for contemplation. The post-war world rejected subtlety and the new drawings duly recorded the fact. Children leaped into Heaven. Mermaids taught their children to swim amidst pounding waves. Children romped in the woods, and Night came billowing downwards to envelop Day.

As before, most of the drawings were done on vellum. The creamy ground gave a greater strength to many of the colours, especially the white of blossom and the gold and silver which could be burnished and made to glitter. Mercurial scarlet and purple resounded with pomp and pageantry, and the blues made the skies more Mediterranean than Scottish. The strong colours gave Jessie's work a force that the subject matter was sometimes too feeble to support, but the results were, nevertheless, exciting and compelling. Jessie still preferred to illustrate literary subjects but, whereas many of the early drawings had touched on arcane themes, the new ones illustrated stories, songs and poems intended specifically for children. She drew anything that took her fancy, often picking out an isolated scene from a story without ever intending to illustrate the complete work. The drawings always included a quotation from the text but there was rarely mention of the title, and an 'Elsa' or a 'Bimbo' in the caption often poses intriguing questions of provenance.

The lettering in the new quotations was coarser than in the old ones. Once it had been an integral part of the decoration, as important to the unity as the inscription by a Japanese artist. Now it was little more than a label. Each word was still separated from its fellows by a star or a dot, but the new block capitals were more solid, yet more unobtrusive, than the old ones. The message had become more important than the decorative content. The capital 'O' no longer sheltered under the arm of a 'T' or in the fork of an 'F'. The extended stems of the 'I' no longer rose tall and proud from the surrounding alphabetical jungle. Now the letters were uniform in size, drawn with the brush rather than with the pen. The new lettering was better suited to the more extroverted style, for subtle penwork would have looked incongruous in the new pictures. The bluntness did not represent a loss of technique or a compensation for failing eyesight; rather, it was a deliberate attempt by the artist to match her style to her new message in the light of the times in which she was living.

CHAPTER TWELVE

Pottery and Murals

Towards the end of 1919, leaving Merle with Mary at Kirkcudbright, Jessie and Ernest went over to Paris to find out for themselves whether there was any future for them there. What they saw confirmed the stories they had heard about the collapse of artistic life in the city and the destruction of the surrounding countryside. The Paris Salon was opening again the following April and Jessie arranged to show some of her drawings and a batik panel 'The Sirens', but both she and Ernest realised that they had to go back to Kirkcudbright, at least until the situation in Paris had improved. Sorting out their possessions they salvaged what they could after four years of disuse, and organised packers to ship their goods to Scotland. They decided not to give up the apartment itself but to keep it as a base for Ernest when he went over on commissions for *The Studio*, and for the eventual use of Merle when, as they hoped, she went to live in Paris to study art.

In another attempt to boost their income Jessie started to decorate pottery again. In the 1920s and 1930s middle-class ladies with artistic

143
Jessie M. King's pottery mark, circa 1935. Decorated teacup.

144
Jessie M. King, 'Sunshine of Saint Eulalie', circa 1927. Pen, ink and watercolour. 33 cm. × 48.3 cm. Private collection.

145
Jessie M. King, 'Gathering Flowers', circa 1925. Pen, ink and watercolour. 31.7 cm. × 43.2 cm.

WRAP THY FORM IN A MANTLE GREY STAR - IN WROVGHT
BLIND WITH THINE HAIR THE EYES OF DAY

146 *Jessie M. King, illustration for 'Ode to Night', circa 1926, by Shelley. Pen, ink and watercolour. 35.5 cm × 30.5 cm. Private collection.*

pretensions painted pottery, much as they had done watercolours a generation before, and were to do flower arranging a generation after. Many art dealers stocked blanks and organised kilns to fire their customers' work. Jessie's supplier was David Methven's pottery at Kirkcaldy, in Fife. Regular shipments of blanks, of painted biscuit, and of fired and finished ware passed between Kirkcaldy and Kirkcudbright by train and carrier's horse and cart until the firm eventually closed down in 1928. At first Jessie used standard blanks of plates, bowls and mugs, and decorated them in underglaze with large semi-abstract floral designs in blue, purple and black. Later she had Methven make special blanks to her own designs of jugs, vases and dishes of various kinds. She recorded details of one of these shipments in the back of one of her sketchbooks: '5 Toby jugs, 5 mugs, 2 large plates, 1 small flat plate, 8 nappies (i.e. napkin rings), 9 ditto with flat border, 8 bowls large, 6 bowls small, 5 eggcups, 1 vase.' She ground her own colours from blocks of pigment that a Paris foundry shipped over for her, but she came to find that, although the underglaze colours were strong and durable, they often altered in the firing and the final colours could not be predicted. She changed to overglaze colours which, though less durable, gave more consistent results, especially when matched sets had to be made. On the base of every one of her pieces Jessie painted her legend of a rabbit, her initials and a green gate, which sometimes turned black in the firing. At the beginning, too, she dated her best pieces but discontinued the practice when her output increased and became less manageable.

Most of Jessie's decorations were of stylised flowers, with bluebells, forget-me-nots, pansies and campions spread round the rim of porridge bowls or dotted round the outside of teacups. Some, though, were complete illustrations in themselves. A small lidded jar she painted in 1922 had illustrations from Maeterlinck's *The Blue Bird*. She did a 'Little Mermaid' vase and, on her largest work, an 'Ali Baba' vase, she included every one of the forty thieves. She did many scenes with elves and rabbits at play, some of them with captions like her book illustrations. She had the ability of the true ceramic artist of being able to relate her design to the shape of the object she was working on, rather than making a flat picture that would then be bent round a mug or a plate.

Jessie had several shows of her pottery at the Glasgow Society of Lady Artists. She sold many items at these exhibitions and received a number of commissions to make individual pieces for private customers. The main outlet for her pottery was the Paul Jones Tea Room in Kirkcudbright. John Paul Jones, of local notoriety, was regarded as a pirate in this country and a hero in the United States. He had been locked up in Kirkcudbright Tolbooth for an alleged offence while serving in the Royal Navy, and had gone on to become the founder of the American Navy. Jessie had designed the sign for the tea rooms in the form of a ship's prow protruding from the wall, with a figure-head at its bowsprit and stylised waves painted on the sides. She had also designed the menu in navy blue with a portrait of Paul Jones in white on the cover, and the pirate costumes for the waitresses made up of red and white chequered pirate shirts, navy skirts, red kerchiefs and earrings of brass curtain rings. In exchange the Taylors were allowed to have their pottery and pictures on sale in the rooms. The pottery proved very popular and most of the homes in Kirkcudbright still contain some item of Jessie M. King's work—now no longer in the kitchen cupboard for everyday use but locked away as a prized ornament and work of art in the china cabinet.

The biggest boost to the Taylors' rather uncertain income came in 1921 when Jessie was made the first recipient of the Lauder Award of the Glasgow Society of Lady Artists and, somewhat bemused, she was presented with a cheque for £250 for the best work in the annual exhibition. She was also invited, along with Ernest, to design wrappers again for Gowans & Gray. Ernest's designs, although beautifully structured, were rather sombre, often with heavy bars of black separating his colours in the manner of his stained-glass work. Jessie's covers were much more free and decorative, more so even than her pre-war designs. She used no modelling and a minimum of perspective. A figure was nearer because it was in front of another, not because of any feeling of depth behind. The hard colours Jessie used reinforced the two-dimensional effect and, with the background showing through the segmented figures, the effect was one of puppets made out of coloured card, and this added to the gaiety of the designs.

Jessie M. King was also one of the artists who were invited in 1923 to contribute to the Queen's Dolls' House. This was an immense project intended as a tribute to Queen Mary, and consisted of a miniature palace, designed by Sir Edwin Lutyens, and decorated, carpeted, furnished and fitted exactly to scale with every conceivable item that might have been found in a full-sized residence of that kind. Everything worked, from a minute electric lift and a petrol-driven lawn mower, to a wind-up gramophone with a tiny record made specially by His Master's Voice. There was a large library of beautifully bound miniature books, many written specially for the occasion, and a collection of paintings, drawings and prints commissioned from the most famous artists in the country. Jessie M. King's watercolour, 'The Little Mermaid', only 1 in. × 1 in. in size, was housed in a special cabinet of drawings alongside works by Brangwyn, William Orpen and Arthur Rackham. There was no fee but, like her fellow contributors, Jessie had the honour of a personal letter of thanks from Queen Mary herself.

By 1925, as a result of his many articles for *The Studio*, E. A. Taylor had come to be recognised as an authority on the contemporary art scene. The publicity brought him several inquiries from prospective pupils, an invitation to become visiting lecturer at a new private art school in London, and a commission to design the whole interior of the new five-storey Inverness Restaurant at Dumfries. By October 1925 he had so much work in hand that he had to turn down an offer from Collins to decorate a new series of poetry books. These 'Dorian Booklets' were an attempt to revive the old 'sweetheart' type of miniature gift book. On Taylor's recommendation, Jessie was offered the commission. She designed a title page featuring a modernised version of her contemplative lady of the bookplates, and endpapers with a woodland scene of poets and minstrels performing for a little princess. The drawing was simple and stylised but it echoed Jessie's earlier work in the expressiveness of the arms and hands of her figures.

Collins immediately commissioned her to design two pictorial covers for

147
Jessie M. King, 'The Little Mermaid', 1923. Illustration for the Queen's Dolls' House. 2.5 cm. × 2.5 cm. H.M. The Queen.

148
Jessie M. King, 'As I was walking all Alane', circa 1933. Illustration for The Twa Corbies. *Pen, ink and coloured inks. 25.4 cm. × 19.7 cm. Private collection.*

AS·I·WAS·WALKING·ALL·ALANE·
HEARD·TWA·CORBIES·MAKIN'·THEIR·
MANE·THE·YIN·VNTO·THE·TITHER·DID·SAY -
WHAVR·SALL·WE·GANG·AND·DINE·THIS·
DAY?

149
Jessie M. King, decorated tea service, circa 1933. Teapot height 16.5 cm. Private collection.

150 *Jessie M. King, 'Ali Baba', Vase, circa 1934. Height 39.5 cm. Private collection.*

151
Jessie M. King, 'Jacobite Lays', cover design, 1928. (Golden Dawn Booklets). Pen, ink and watercolour.

their 'Bumper Rewards', a new series of children's books. Jessie's designs were used arbitrarily over a variety of titles and, although a picture of children reading in a garden made a suitable cover for Mrs Henry Wood's *Danesbury House*, it was somewhat disconcerting to find an edition of *Alice in Wonderland* cased in a richly coloured scene of a knight in armour pointing to an Arabian camel train travelling by moonlight through a grove of poplars. A third commission from Collins followed in 1927 for the cover and endpapers of a further series of poetry books, the 'Golden Dawn Booklets'. This time Jessie took the title of the series as her theme and showed a young girl in a soft dress dancing to the glory of a new day, drawn, most suitably, in wavy Art Deco lines of red, blue and gold.

Another reason why E. A. Taylor had felt unable to accept Collins' commission was that in the autumn of 1925 he and Jessie had been invited to design the interior decorations for a new experimental nursery school that the Lanarkshire authorities were building at Drumpark for handicapped children. The Taylors were given a free hand, and decided to base their designs on flowers. Ernest chose the colour schemes and Jessie prepared stencilled friezes for the walls, with elves and fairies playing among clusters of 'Primrose', 'Snowdrop', 'Old Rose' and the other flowers that were used as names for the classrooms. In 'Sunflower', for example, elfin soldiers, in armour made of sunflower petals, fought one another by the light of a rising sunflower sun. Jessie paid several visits to the school to get the feel of the siting of the murals and their scale. She made large preliminary sketches of her compositions in charcoal and colour washes and, from these, made detailed paintings in gouache. The actual cutting of the stencils was done under her supervision by the firm of decorators who were painting the school, and she and Ernest attended to the mixing of the colours they had decided on.

It was the first time that children's taste had been given consideration in the planning of a new school. The success of the venture encouraged the Lanarkshire authorities to repeat the experiment the following year at Machen, a new school at Larkhall, and the Taylors were invited again to plan the décor for the seven classrooms for the youngest children. They called the rooms 'Morning', 'Noon', 'Night', 'Spring', 'Summer', 'Autumn' and 'Winter' and, as at Drumpark, they based their decorations on the colours implied by the titles. 'Night', for example, was painted a deep blue and had stencilled designs of princes, princesses and their playfellows in pale blue and white.

The Taylors also designed a number of self-contained panels for the schools. At Machen Jessie painted a group of four panels in watercolour with scenes from *Morte d'Arthur*, and in 1927 Ernest painted a large watercolour for the assembly hall of Dalyell High School, Motherwell showing Columbus's galleon, symbolising youth, setting out on the voyage of discovery of new worlds. Taylor loved to moralise. Another galleon, in oils this time, for a school in Motherwell bore the caption 'He that hath steerage of my course direct my sails', and yet another, in painted gesso for a school at Morningside, Edinburgh, bore the rather ambiguous homily 'For mercy, courage, kindness, mirth/There is no measure upon earth'. Jessie painted one of her few oils, *Little Brown Seed*, for Drumpark School, but her finest work for the Lanarkshire authorities was a group that she did for Mossend School of seven

154 *Jessie M. King. Brochure for Girl Guides Pageant, 1927. 10.7 cm. × 45.7 cm.*

152
Jessie M. King. Cover design for Alice in Wonderland *by Lewis Carroll. Published by Collins 1927.*

153
Jessie M. King. Cover design for Danesbury House *by Mrs Henry Wood. Published by Collins 1927. Pen, ink and watercolour.*

155 Jessie M. King, three panels designed for Mossend School, Lanarkshire, 1928. Opposite 'Piper Play', top, 'How the Queen went A-maying', 'How Four Queens Found Sir Launcelot.' Pen, ink and bodycolour on vellum. Strathclyde Department of Education.

gouache panels illustrating the story of Sir Lancelot. The series included scenes, such as 'Elaine gives Sir Launcelot the Embroidered Sleeve', that she had never illustrated before, as well as new interpretations of 'How the Queen went a-Maying' and others of her favourite episodes. All the panels were done in pink, white, blues and greens, and had a freshness and gaiety that even the most blinkered child must have found attractive.

The Lanarkshire education authorities planned to redecorate all the schools under their administration along similar lines, and the Taylors looked forward to a lifetime of attractive commissions which would provide them with a steady income and would combine artistic satisfaction with public good. But the collapse of the stock market, the General Strike and the depression of the 1930s put an end to such good intentions and, with it, the hopes of the Taylors.

Jessie spent much of the spring of 1927 organising a large pageant for the Girl Guides of all the towns and villages around Kirkcudbright. She personally undertook the immense task of designing and arranging every float and tableau. Each one illustrated a local legend or a passage from local history. Some were representations of the coats of arms of the towns, with a reluctant Merle enrolled as St Cuthbert of Kirkcudbright. Others featured events in the lives of historical characters who had links with the region. There were scenes from the *Waverley* novels and items as esoteric as the presentation of the charter of Balliol College in 1294 by Devorgilla, Lady of Galloway. A young female Robert Bruce with burnt cork moustaches stared at her cardboard spider. James IV died over and over again at Flodden, and the last witch to be burned in Kirdcudbright shrieked in defiant agony as her float passed through the streets.

Jessie had now established a pattern in organising her pageants. Whenever she saw a suitable candidate she flattered and convinced her victim that she had been born solely for the purpose of attaining the glory that would come about when she took part in Jessie's pageant. She was as persuasive with the parents as she was with the children, and enlisted them as dressmakers and alteration hands. Over the years she had accumulated odd lengths of material. She draped what she thought suitable over the child and presented its parent with detailed instructions of how to convert the fabric into a knight's surcoat or a crofter's breeches. She reviewed her troops at a dress rehearsal, making sure that her sewing ladies were on hand to carry out last-minute alterations. She also designed brochures for her pageants. The one for the Guides took the form of a long panorama, with all the historical characters lined up in procession, and a cast-list inside of all the participants, so that even the smallest Brownie knew that she had been held important.

It was becoming increasingly obvious to Jessie and Ernest that the Paris studio was now more a liability than an asset. Ernest used it only when he had an assignment from *The Studio*, and when, in 1928, Merle asserted her independence and announced that she wanted to read English at Glasgow University, her parents went over to Paris and reluctantly disposed of the atelier and its remaining contents. Ernest continued to visit Paris from time to time to survey the art scene for the magazine, but most of his work related of

Scotland, and he had now been given the greater responsibility for coordinating the reports from all the Scottish art centres. In 1928 he wrote an article for the magazine on some new landscapes Jessie had done. He described how she now preferred to use coloured drawing inks straight from the bottle to mixing her own watercolours from solid blocks, and showed how rich the results were in a reproduction of one of her pictures of their cottage on Arran entitled 'The Fairy Tale House in Real Life'. He commented, 'The realist may be inclined to suggest that such colours do not exist there and have doubts about the fairy-tale house too, but I can assure any doubtful ones that the house does; I have spent some of the happiest days of my life in it, and as for the colour—it exists too but perhaps not in all minds or for all eyes.' Jessie used the coloured inks to great effect in the watercolours she submitted each year for exhibition at the Glasgow Institute, the Royal Scottish Academy and at Liverpool. Illustrations such as 'How beautiful are thy feet' and 'As I was walking all alane', a later version of 'The Twa Corbies', sang out with the boldness of the new colours. She achieved the same effect in the illustrations she did in 1929 for a new book, *Mummy's Bedtime Story Book*, written by an author who used the nom de plume 'Marion', a coincidental linking with Jessie's own name which has caused confusion ever since. The stories were all about good little girls and horrid little boys and their adventures with Jack Frost, Santa Claus and other characters. Every page had pictures and decorations in the new colours and each one glowed with a strength and luminosity worthy of a Matisse.

Many of Jessie's admirers were reluctant to accept the changes that had taken place in her style. They were ready to applaud work that had been painstakingly done and looked technically dexterous, but they felt cheated by the new, simple statements. Jessie's new forms and the use of what, at first sight, appeared to be unsubtle colour, her 'strong drink', as she called it, were received with murmurs of disappointment. A more enlightened response came in a review in the *Glasgow Bulletin* of an exhibition of her work at the Glasgow Society of Lady Artists in 1930. The critic remarked on the tendency towards disparagement of Jessie's new work and wrote 'Jessie M. King shows a delightful sense of arrangement and happy colour in her large and imaginatively treated picture 'Heard Melodies are Sweet'. It is unnecessary to criticise the drawing—any matter-of-fact person can do that—the thing is to appreciate the vision.'

In an exhibition *Spring in Three Rooms* which Jessie M. King and Helen Paxton Brown held jointly in April 1931, they showed how this 'happy colour' could transform interior decoration. Each room was given a brilliantly coloured carpet as a foundation: orange, vivid blue and heliotrope in turn. In the orange room were specimens of embroidery by Nell Brown and curtains designed by Jessie, some in batik and others embroidered to her designs. In the blue room tables were laid with Jessie's painted crockery as 'Breakfast for Four', 'Supper for Six' and 'The Children have Tea'. In the third room, on the heliotrope carpet were two suites of bedroom furniture made specially to the artists' designs and painted in plain bright colours in a novel departure from the more usual dark veneered or stained wood. Nell Brown's suite was in daffodil yellow and Jessie's in cream and green with an orange rabbit painted

156
*Jessie M. King, 'The
Sleeping Beauty', circa 1929.
Pen, ink and watercolour
on vellum.
31.7 cm × 16.5 cm. Private
collection.*

on the head and foot of the bed. Over it was a linen frieze with one of the elf-and-fairy motifs she had used in the schools, and around the walls were watercolours by Nell Brown and some of Jessie's illustrations of fairy tales and nursery poetry. The whole effect was cheerful and light-hearted, sufficient to banish the gloom of any sad child. The critic of the *Glasgow Evening News* appreciated the novelty of the bedroom suites and commented on 'the beauty yet to be fully exploited in painted furniture'. If no commissions for bright modern furniture came out of the exhibition, Jessie was consoled by two letters she received from their friend Gordon Bottomley. In one, praising her work in general he wrote 'In the great Romantic flowering of the time of our youth there is no one with a more authentic place than you: there are no other artists with a natural creative gift more original than your own . . . I wonder where you came from!' And in the other, thanking her for a copy of *Budding Life*, he wrote, 'You are a jeweller, a silversmith, a gardener good at both flowers and nectarines, a mistress mariner on pearly seas in fairy lands unborn.'

CHAPTER THIRTEEN

Talks and Toys

For several years E. A. Taylor had been urging *The Studio* to publish an article that would help reawaken public interest in Charles Rennie Mackintosh, whose unique contribution to architecture and design had been shamefully neglected after the First World War. Geoffrey Holme, the editor of the magazine and Fra Newbery, who from his retirement at Corfe Castle in Dorset, wrote of Mackintosh as 'a genius that one could dream about', both offered to help, but disputes with Margaret Macdonald, the artist's widow, about the content of the article, delayed its publication. Mackintosh had died in December 1928, but a suitable tribute to his achievements was not made until 1933, after Margaret's death, when a large memorial exhibition was held in Glasgow. Taylor himself eventually wrote the article and described a chance meeting with Mackintosh on Arran before the turn of the century. 'I watched him draw those trunks,' he wrote, 'with a thin nervous line, and colour them in with black ink, and the grass a pure unshadowed green.' Taylor mentioned particularly Mackintosh's later landscapes and flower paintings which the critics had always dismissed as trivial. He remarked that, even in the great days of Mackintosh's influence in Europe, his genius had never been fully appreciated in Great Britain, and gave as an example a book by H.J. Jennings, published in London in 1902 entitled *Our Homes and How to Beautify Them*, in which the only illustration of a work by Mackintosh had been in a section on 'Hooliganism in Art'.

Jessie, too, was invited from time to time to write and lecture on various aspects of art. On two occasions, once in a lecture to the Glasgow Society of Lady Artists and, more fully in 1933, in a series of talks organised by the Dumfries and Galloway Fine Art Society, where she regularly exhibited, she spoke on book illustration. In her opinion an illustrator was born, not made. She held that the fanciful pictures that the mind made when it was confronted with a poem or a story were things that could never be taught. Only the technique of how to convert these mental pictures into artistic statements could be developed by formal training. She told how she admired the work of Aubrey Beardsley, Phil May and many of the French illustrators, especially Boutet de Monvel, whose ability to balance text and illustration was, she felt, beyond criticism. She maintained that real book illustration needed more than the faultless recording of images, and that the illustrator had to have a sense of design before his craft could be considered as an art. She explained how she divided book illustrators into the 'naturalists' who drew things as they knew they should be, and what she called the 'symbolist throng' to which she herself

SHE·WAS·BUSY·ALL·DAY·LONG···
AND·OFTEN·ALL·NIGHT·AS·WELL·

157 Jessie M. King, 'She was busy all day long', 1929. Illustration for 'Marion', Mummy's
Bedtime Story Book. Coloured inks.

158 Jessie M. King, 'How beautiful are thy feet', circa 1935. Pen and coloured inks on vellum.
31.7 cm. × 16.5 cm. Private collection.

belonged. She said that every illustrator had a particular area in which he felt most at home, and that one could no more visualise Arthur Rackham doing illustrations for *Redgauntlet* than she herself doing Dickens. She spoke of her attitude towards book design. 'To put a naturalistic looking cottage with a very natural sky and windswept trees on the cover of a book and call it *Our Village* is not a method of decoration. The plain cover with a well-placed title would represent what I think would be a decorated page. To take your naturalist form and treat it with your own imagination and place the results on the cover—there you come to the land of decoration. A page of type, beautifully set, a little ornament beautifully surrounded by type, a chapter heading, symbolic or treating of the matter in the chapter and summing up in it something of the whole trend of thought in that chapter, is to me what book Decoration means.' She went on to describe her own guidelines: 'How can I transform picture into decoration? How can I simplify? How can I convey the essence with the minimum amount of information? In short, how can I tell everything without showing everything?'

Jessie believed that children were the best illustrators and the most cruel critics because their inspiration came from their imagination rather than their memory of what they had seen. 'As you read,' she said, 'the pictures pass behind your head, in my case from the back of the right-hand side of my head just like on a cinema film, sometimes vague at first but gradually assuming concrete form, and it is as they take on that more tangible aspect that I trap them and fit them on my parchment.' She felt that children had the same faculty. She pointed out how children will often keep up a running commentary as they draw of what is queuing up in their heads to come out. She described the powerful effect of illustration on the reader and gave instance of how, for a long time, her own vision of Hell had been based on the woodcut illustrations in an old copy of *The Pilgrim's Progress* she had owned as a child. 'Some day,' she said, 'I hope to illustrate *The Pilgrim's Progress*, but for years Hell meant to me a weird coloured drawing among a set of Bible pictures where horrid and dark coloured devils shoved fair-haired and white-skinned men and women into a hole in the ground from which flames issued. Now that I am growing up, in bits, I think it is a place with red velvet pile carpets and red embossed wallpaper of acanthus leaves, the inner chamber is shelved all round, with glasses of hot milk, my pet aversion, sitting on the shelves. People, not even horned, sweep the carpets from which come clouds of red dust. At intervals they cease sweeping and the dust is allowed to settle on the glasses of hot milk and then, as they sweep again, other people make you drink it for ever and ever.'

For a long time Jessie had wanted to record Kirkcudbright as she had done Glasgow and Edinburgh. Foulis, who had published the other two 'City' books, no longer existed as an independent company but in 1934 Gowans & Gray, who had published her book on Culross, took up the idea. Jessie produced some eighteen drawings of old buildings and closes in the town, all in the freer style of her more recent work. Again, she tried to capture not only the anatomy of the buildings but the atmosphere of the scene so that, for example, she deliberately foreshortened the drawing of Greengate Close and made the walls of the cottages slope inwards to emphasise their protective

159
Jessie M. King, 'Behind the Tolbooth', 1934. Illustration from Kirkcudbright A Royal Burgh *published by Gowans & Gray. Pen and ink. 14.6 cm. × 10.1 cm.*

character. She included two drawings of the Tolbooth, one from the High Street and the other from the gardens at the back where, as all the artists knew, there was a better composition. She drew Hornel's home, Broughton House, with its fine steps and gate; Gordon Anderson's mysterious smithy, and the old cottage by the harbour that later became an art gallery. As a tailpiece she drew the 'Bridestone' which was once set in the wall of a house in the High Street and which recorded the fact that in 1666 'I. B. had been betrothed to E. M. C.' The house itself had recently been demolished and Ernest had saved the stone. In a preliminary drawing Jessie drew the stone in isolation but in the final drawing for the book she returned it to its rightful place in the wall.

The drawings for the Kirkcudbright book were in black and white but,

BRAN·SETS·SAIL·FOR·THE·ISLES

like many of the ones Jessie was doing at the time, they seemed to have been
conceived in terms of colour. They were made up of numerous islets
which, like the outlines in a child's painting book, invited colouring in. In
Kirkcudbright the islets were shaded in various ways, not to provide
modelling but to enhance the decorative aspect. In other drawings of the time,
such as those she did between 1931 and 1935 for *The Gallovidian Annual*,

some of the islets were patterned, a few were in solid black, but most were left white, so that the drawings appeared to describe the skeletal structure of whatever was being depicted. Even the open-face lettering of the captions was made of fine double lines to harmonise with the tone of the drawing. The idiom was essentially Art Deco but, within this, Jessie managed to achieve great flexibility. In 1934, in the illustrations for the new edition of Arthur Corder's *Our Lady's Garland*, despite the wavy lines of sunbeams and the frizzy hair that were part of the language of the style, she captured perfectly the peace and innocence of the poems. When she used colour, as she did in a single watercolour of a quotation from *The Song of Songs*, or in the series of illustrations of little girls playing in flower gardens which she did in 1935 for Florence Drummond's book *The Fringes of Paradise*, she showed that what looked to be a mannerism was, in fact, her brilliant adaptation of the Art Deco idiom to her own philosophy of how a drawing works.

In May 1935 Jessie held another joint exhibition with Helen Paxton Brown at the Glasgow Society of Lady Artists. Entitled 'Youth's the Stuff' it was described by Jessie as 'whimsy'. As well as the usual examples of Nell Brown's embroidery, Jessie's pottery, batik and some little rugs she had done with pictures of 'Spring things', the exhibition contained the first fruits of a new collaboration between Jessie and Tim Jeffs, a sculptor friend of theirs, also from Kirkcudbright. Jessie was still pursuing the idea of manufacturing artist-designed toys. She had seen examples in France designed by Boutet de Monvel and Caran d'Ache, and was convinced that there was a market for such things in this country. Jessie drew several designs and Tim Jeffs made up prototypes for the exhibition. Together they constructed a Noah's Ark with flat, two-dimensional animals, some dolls' houses and a number of tall, free-standing toy soldiers, all painted in bright colours. They also built a replica of McLellan Castle in Kirkcudbright and a canal house which they set over a stream of running water. The Taylors and the Jeffs dreamed of the display being the nucleus of a large co-operative business that would restore all their fortunes and occupy them all in stimulating and profitable work. Jessie prepared a lecture, 'The Wooden Toy', in which she tried to explain her aims and advertise the scheme, but none of them had the capital or the business acumen to promote the project and, as the practical difficulties began to reveal themselves, their enthusiasm waned.

CHAPTER FOURTEEN

Arrivals and Departures

In autumn 1936, shortly after the Taylors had returned from the summer school on Arran, Eva died at the age of sixty-five at her home in Bridge of Weir. She had always been the stable member of the family, quietly spoken and reserved. The nonconformist ways of Adah and Jessie, although amusing to listen to, often left her slightly bewildered, and she had always been rather shocked at the goings on at Greengate. Jessie and she had little in common and had sometimes taken each other for granted, but there had been a deep affection between them and Merle often stayed there when her parents were in Paris. Jessie grieved at this severance of yet another family bond.

In the summer of 1937 Mary McNab, now aged seventy-eight, got an assistant. Young Jessie McCoul was hired to come each morning to help out at Greengate. From the beginning, to avoid the confusion of names, she was called 'Brownie' because of the colour of her overall. She helped Mary with the brasses and the cooking, and assisted Jessie in the batik studio, grinding the colours, stretching the fabric for Jessie to work on, helping to dissolve the excess wax in the aviation spirit they used, and washing the finished fabric in Lux. When Brownie arrived it was agreed that she should be paid weekly. Mary, of course, lived in and was paid when the Taylors had money. Ernest himself was 'above' money and Jessie hardly recognised its existence until the bills mounted up. Every Friday, though, Brownie received an envelope containing 7s 6d. Each week's envelope had a drawing on it in pen or pencil or, sometimes, coloured crayon, in which Jessie illustrated one of the week's happenings and added a humorous caption in her block capitals. Jessie McCoul kept the envelopes and, over the years, assembled a picture diary of her life at Greengate. There were pictures of a Brownie caught in the rain, of a stray cat being chased out of the kitchen, of something broken, or a meal burnt and, for occasions such as Christmas or Easter or St Valentine's Day, there were special drawings of mermaids or flowers or rabbits all bringing greetings appropriate to the event.

Greetings cards were always treated with importance at Greengate. In 1929 Jessie had designed the first of a long series of Christmas and New Year cards for their own use. Originally Ernest and she had planned to take turns in the designing of the cards but Ernest was not very committed to the idea and, over the years, most of them were designed by Jessie. Each card was simple, with perhaps a single figure of a young girl or an elf or a fairy, printed in colour, with a few words of greeting and an occasional exhortation such as 'Put a girdle round the World' or 'Ring in the New'. Taken on their own the

162
Jessie M. King, 'Brownies Good Deed', circa 1937. Pen and ink on paper. 9.5 cm. × 12 cm. Private collection.

163
Jessie M. King, 'March 1st', circa 1938. Pen and ink on paper. 9.5 cm. × 12 cm. Private collection.

cards seemed slight, but they had a consistency of style and a sincerity of purpose that was totally winning so that, seen as a group, they had a particular distinction.

Another household task that Jessie insisted on doing herself was the finishing of the outside steps. Ever since her childhood at Bearsden she had loved to draw on flagstones and cobbles. Once a week, when Brownie had scrubbed the doorsteps, Jessie would get down on her hands and knees and decorate them in pipe-clay with rabbits and flowers, or sometimes just pretty squiggles, to liven up the entrance. She produced her masterpiece in this form in November 1939 when Tom Collin, possibly the first non-artist resident of the Close and future curator of the Stewartry Museum at Kirkcudbright, got married. When he came back from his honeymoon, he and his bride found, as they stepped through the archway leading to the Close, that the cobblestones starting from Jessie's back door and going all the way down to the cottage at the bottom where they were going to live, had been chalked over with hearts and flowers and had, as a centrepiece, a prince leading his princess through the arrows and messages 'To the Blue Door'.

In May 1938 Mary McNab died at the age of seventy-nine. She had been friend, nurse and companion to both Jessie and Merle and had always been looked upon as part of the family. This tiny wiry woman for whom, as a country girl, Glasgow had marked the limits of the world, had accompanied Jessie on her early travels to the continent and had taken the move to Paris in

164
Jessie M. King, 'Ring in the New', greetings card, circa 1937. 20.3 cm. × 13.3 cm.

her stride. Foreigners, she felt, were just another test that the Good Lord had put in the way of the smooth ordering of life. Jessie mourned for her and missed her busy presence in her life. In an attempt to lift her depression Ernest suggested that she go away with Merle and Anna Hotchkiss for a short holiday and so, that June, Jessie went over to Iona for the first time and spent a week there painting and sketching in an attempt to assuage her grief.

165 Jessie M. King. Decorated cobblestones. Greengate Close 1939.

When war broke out in 1939 Merle, who had been working as a medical secretary, joined the WRNS and served for the duration on the south coast. Ernest was now sixty-five and any intention he had of helping with the war effort had to be postponed when, in October, his car slipped from a ramp and crushed his foot. He was admitted to hospital and was not considered fit enough to go about again until the following spring. He spent the war years giving lectures and broadcasts for the Ministry of Information on the progress of the war and on various art topics. He received two guineas a lecture, and both he and Jessie were grateful for even that slight income. The annual summer school had come to an end and, without tourists, and the fact that blanks for decoration were hard to come by, pottery sales were few. Jessie earned a little as a part-time art teacher at Kirkcudbright Academy where she tried to teach not only the rudiments of technique but also how to look at things intelligently. She insisted in her life classes that the children she chose as models should look dishevelled with ruffled hair and wrinkled socks. 'Disorder,' she said, 'is much more interesting than neatness.' She prepared large watercolours of flowers with subsidiary drawings of them broken down into their botanical components in order to teach the children how to structure their drawings. She set up still-lifes and made the pupils paint the spaces between the objects and look for colour in the shadows. 'Whenever in doubt,' she told them, 'do it in purple.'

There were few visitors to Greengate during the Second World War.

Adah, who had been teaching in Paris, came back to Scotland in 1939 as war seemed imminent, but returned to Paris during the first months of the 'phoney war' to sort out her affairs. She was caught up in the German advance and arrested. After a period of interrogation she was released and allowed to go and live with friends in Versailles. She managed to get a letter through to Jessie in September 1941 in which she offered to help them financially and authorised the Taylors to draw on her bank account in Kirkcudbright. She seemed cheerful and optimistic but was arrested again, shortly afterwards, and interned in a concentration camp under horrifying conditions for the rest of the war. One new friend that the Taylors made in Kirkcudbright on account of the war was the young Ronald Searle who had been called up into the army straight from Cambridge. Taylor noticed him in uniform one day sketching and invited him home. Searle found Greengate a haven of sympathy, and his evenings with Jessie and Ernest helped him to adjust to the sudden contrast of army life. Through the Taylors he met Miles Johnston who had a studio in Castle Street, and it was the Johnston daughters in their school uniforms who were the models for the first St Trinian's girls.

Towards the end of the war Jessie was asked to illustrate a children's picture book, *The Enchanted Capital of Scotland*, which described the wonderful things a party of children discovered on a school trip to Edinburgh. Jessie made the whole book one huge extended design with drawings weaving in and out of the text in the way that her model, Boutet de Monvel, used to do. She filled each page with flowers, butterflies, elves, children and the architectural marvels of the city. Interspersed were double-page illustrations in bright cerise, purple, pink and chrome-yellow that glowed against the areas of white space. She drew the city as a child might see it, without perspective or modelling, capturing the feeling of wonder that the unsophisticated visitors must have had on first seeing the sights there. Everything, though, was carefully planned and Jessie made many preliminary drawings for the book. The illustrations still showed links with her past work. Tree trunks were made up of separate panels, like areas of camouflage, just as they had been in the Paris drawings. There was the same hatching on buildings as in the first 'City' books, and even a halo could be seen here and there on some of the characters. To finish off the book and remind the world that she was still active, Jessie included a little drawing of herself on the title-page as a witch on a broomstick, wearing her buckled shoes and black hat, and carrying, in place of a magic wand, her brushes and palette.

On Victory Day in 1945 Jessie organised the last, and what she claimed was the best, of her Kirkcudbright pageants. Once again she picked her characters from the people she met in the street. 'You might be a student in the sixth form,' she told one young lady, 'but to me you are Flora Macdonald.' It was a Royal command. She organised volunteers from the Scouts and Guides, the Women's Institute and the various church societies, and trained each group separately. Because petrol was still rationed she charmed the commanding officer of the local army camp into lending her six lorries to carry the tableaux ,and arranged for them to travel behind the band of little 'walkers' at the front in case some small elf faltered. She kept to her favourite themes of Scottish Ballads, Walter Scott and Burns, and brought in allegories

166
Left to right: Jessie M. King, Maime and Merle, circa 1938.

167
Caricature of Jessie by 'W', July 1938. Pen and ink. 14 cm. × 8.8 cm.

168
Jessie M. King, 'Common House Leek', circa 1941. Charcoal and watercolour on paper. 107.9 cm. × 55.8 cm. Private collection.

169
Jessie M. King, 'Riding the Marches', 1947. Pen and ink on vellum.

of the victory of Good over Evil. There was, however, no Britannia because Jessie detested the woman. On the great day the procession of floats, led by its little green troup, started from the Tolbooth on a circuit of the town, with Jessie in her saint's costume darting from place to place making sure her charges were keeping in battle order. The pageant was a triumph but, when it was all over, an exhausted Jessie wrote a letter of abdication: 'I the undersigned, Jessie M. King, do hereby agree never to handle a pageant or anything remotely connected with fancy dress from this date of signature as witness my signature this fifteenth day of May 1945.' On the left of the page she drew a shield with a Greengate rabbit in the centre and the motto *Lapin Couchant* around it. On the right, surrounding a drawing of a bell and her gate symbol, she wrote 'And the Raven said Never more shall it ring for Costume at Greengate'. And she made the document official with a twopenny stamp. She kept her vow, breaking it only slightly when, in 1947, she illustrated a brochure for the old-established Dumfries pageant of Riding the Marches, which commemorated the granting of the Royal Charter to that city in the Middle Ages.

After the war Jessie and Ernest felt that they no longer had the energy to start up the summer school again. A photograph of Jessie taken in 1946, when she was seventy-one, showed her sitting in the garden at Greengate wearing a velvet jacket and her famous hat. Her hair was now white and her eyes had a soft benevolent look that made her seem at peace with life. Even in old age she was determined that nobody should see her wearing spectacles out of doors. She no longer appeared eccentric. The Queen of the Corbies—'The Raven', as she referred to herself—had become the embodiment of everyone's dream of a fairy godmother, possessed of the secrets of age-old wisdom. When reconstruction started after the war Jessie was invited to paint two large pictures for the dining room of a new school at Dalbeattie. Like Ernest, she

believed in the traditional values of faith and honour, and decided to illustrate two exhortatory messages to modern youth. The first one, using Arthur Hugh Clough's poem 'Where lies the land to where this ship must go?', showed the adventurousness of youth, with a family in ancient Scottish dress watching a little ship with sails of many colours, and birds flying about the rigging, setting off for unknown lands. The other illustration, in Jessie's favourite colours of yellow and blue, was inscribed 'The Golden Age is not past, it is Now'. It pictured an arcadian scene with human beings and dryads gathered round a tree. Tiny birds set in discs of gold flew about their heads and, as if to bring her life's work full circle, Jessie gave the main figure a halo of bluebirds swooping inwards towards the centre, just as she had done so very long ago for Siddhartha.

by JAMES McCARDEL, D.D.

*171
Jessie M. King, 'The Parish
of New Kilpatrick', 1949.
Cover design. Coloured
inks and watercolour.*

In May 1949 Jessie went over to Bearsden to make notes for the cover design of a book entitled *The Parish of New Kilpatrick*, which included a section on her father's incumbency. It was to be her last work and, rightly, it took her back to the place where her enthusiasm for art had begun. The visit was especially poignant because she had just heard of the death of Adah in Versailles where she had gone to live after her release from the concentration camp. The watercolour Jessie painted of the church seen through the trees at the bottom of the Manse garden was very simple and seemed an embodiment of Jessie's belief that only in the early part of one's life does one need accumulation and elaboration. At the end one has to discard and refine.

A last photograph of Jessie showed her standing outside Greengate waving cheerily as the wind fussed her hair. At the end of July she had a heart attack and died on 3 August 1949 at the age of seventy-three. By her wish she was cremated and her ashes were taken by Ernest up to Strachur at the head of Loch Fyne to be scattered over Mary's grave. A memorial service was held in Kirkcudbright at which her humanity was stressed, and the spirit of the child in her acknowledged as the source of her understanding of suffering and her deep compassion. She was affectionately described as having been a law unto herself in the town, original in everything she did and generous of her talent. From her citizenship, it was rightly said, Kirkcudbright had gained real distinction.

The strength of the Taylors' marriage had been in their tolerance of each other's foibles and their unbounded generosity of spirit. Each appreciated this quality in the other. Amongst Ernest's papers after his death two years later was found a note in his handwriting headed 'J. M. K. T.' with the following verse:

> She doeth little kindnesses
> which most leave undone or despise,
> for nought that sets one heart at ease,
> or giveth happiness or peace,
> is low esteemed in her eyes.

It was this generosity that was the foundation of the many friendships they made, and it was reflected in the letters of condolence Ernest received. The playwright James Bridie wrote, 'I suppose that one of the most perfect and delightful companionships that ever happened between two human beings has gone to another place. At least, if Jessie has gone into another dimension it is one that she has always known and she will be perfectly at home in it.'

Not long before Jessie's death Bridie had written her a note of thanks for putting him up at Greengate: 'It is common knowledge that you and E. A. Taylor are the two kindest people in the whole world and that you are kind for the fun of the thing and not because you want crowns of glory or thanks or anything like that. You must have put a golden patch into the crazy quilt of many a precious life.' The Revd John White, who had married them, paid testimony to Jessie's goodness in a letter to Ernest: 'God endowed Jessie M. King with great gifts. She created with her vivid imagination a world that moved around herself, and peopled it with the figures of her rich and prolific fancies. Many of her creations are recorded in her pictures, but Jessie M. King

172 *Jessie M. King, 'Magic', circa 1937. Pen, ink and watercolour on vellum. 32.5 cm. × 17.5 cm. Private collection.*

was, in her own life, more wonderful than what her canvases reveal—she was a handmaiden of God who loved her fellow folk and was always happiest when she could help them, counting not the cost to herself.'

There was one posthumous echo. Three of Jessie's works were included in the annual exhibition of the Glasgow Institute that autumn. One of these was a watercolour, 'Magic', that she had done some years earlier. It was a delicate fantasy in turquoise and blue of a young girl, her eyes closed in ecstasy, suspended horizontally between earth, air and a surrounding pool—a creature who, like Jessie herself, belonged to all the elements and existed outside time itself.

173
Jessie M. King at
Greengate, circa 1949.

Epilogue

Jessie M. King's death was not reported in any of the English newspapers. The main Scottish ones merely identified her as 'the wife of the well known painter E. A. Taylor'. The *Dumfries and Galloway Standard*, her local paper, described her as 'Mrs Ernest A. Taylor . . . who painted under her maiden name of Jessie M. King'. At the beginning of this century, when Jessie had an international reputation, few people had heard of E. A. Taylor. At the time of her death the position was completely reversed. Compared with her husband's work Jessie's was almost totally neglected.

After Jessie's death Ernest stayed on at Greengate, and Jessie McCoul, now married, came to live in the Close to help look after him. He painted a little and continued to give the occasional lecture, but the zest was gone from his life and he aged considerably in appearance. He too suffered a heart attack and died in November 1951 at the age of seventy-eight. Like Jessie he was cremated and his ashes were taken north to be strewn near those of his wife. In an obituary notice the *Dumfries and Galloway Standard* commented: 'The arts flourished in Kirkcudbright with the coming of the Taylors. And so an association of some forty years with the town is severed and the loss in artistic, literary and dramatic spheres will be considerable.'

Greengate and the Close still stand, duller perhaps than in Jessie's day. Over the now faded green door that leads from the High Street to the Close there is a commemorative plaque that Charles Oppenheimer, who had come up to live in Kirkcudbright on Ernest's recommendation many years before, had put up. It records, in letters not unlike Jessie's own, with a little dot between each word, the simple fact that 'E. A. Taylor and Jessie M. King Lived and Worked in this House'.

174
Greengate, Kirkcudbright.

Inevitably there has been a reappraisal of Jessie M. King's work. In 1971 the Scottish Arts Council mounted a large retrospective exhibition in which her drawings, books and craftwork of all kinds were shown. Other exhibitions were organised by the National Library of Scotland in 1971 and 1978, and by the Fine Art Society in 1977. In June 1977 the residue of Jessie's studio was put up for auction in Glasgow, and enthusiasts came from all over the world to attend this unique display of art by Jessie M. King and E. A. Taylor. Lot after lot showed the astonishing range of Jessie's talent in book illustration and decoration, and the design of toys, greetings cards, bookplates and murals. There were dozens of the Paris drawings, and watercolours of Galloway and Arran, with preliminary sketches and finished examples of works that had long been familiar to her followers. The Jessie M. King items in the sale fetched

175
Ann MacBeth, title-page for
'The Book of the Jubilee',
1901. Pen and purple ink
heightened with gold.
22.2 cm. × 13.9 cm.

prices far beyond expectation, to an extent that Merle, who was present, expressed disgust at a world in which people could pay such sums for even trivia. By contrast the watercolours and oil paintings of E. A. Taylor went for very little and many remained unsold. Fashion, as always, had its cynical last word.

Jessie M. King's art was a lesser art because it was essentially decorative. Great art must offer insight into the human condition. Decoration, by definition, must be superficial. Nevertheless, in her chosen field of illustration she stood out among her contemporaries. Hilary Evans, writing in *Studio International* in 1968 described Jessie M. King as 'after Beardsley perhaps the finest black and white artist of the period'. As an illustrator Jessie M. King was an idealist. She created a work of art which paralleled, rather than mirrored, the incident she was illustrating. She did not try to enter into the mind of the author. She drew on the feelings that the author's work roused in her. And, as an idealist, she had no need to be slavishly realistic in either anatomy, dress or scenery. Magic is what transforms reality.

Of her contemporaries, only Ann Macbeth, Annie French, Katherine Cameron and Cecile Walton applied themselves with any intensity to book design and decoration. Ann Macbeth (1875–1948), like Jessie, was capable of producing structured decorations for book bindings or preliminaries. She too used the Glasgow grid pattern into which she incorporated typical motifs of lanceolate leaves, blown roses and the lettering peculiar to the Stylists. Her drawing, though, was stiff—something which was true of so many of the Glasgow students, and she lacked Jessie's ability to depart from a rigid prototype, so that stylisation became a refuge from anatomical accuracy. She had a remarkable colour sense and great feeling for design. Her strength lay in needlework and, whilst still a student, she was appointed assistant to Jessie Newbery who was in charge of the needlework department at the school. On Jessie M. King's retirement to get married she took over her post in the Department of Book Design.

Annie French (1872–1965) was the only other of Jessie's contemporaries to specialise in illustrative art. Although she illustrated only one book—a selection of Heine's poems for Foulis in 1908, and contributed to one other—*The Book of the Jubilee of the University of Glasgow* in 1901, her watercolours and drawings were mainly in the form of illustrations. Like Jessie she designed a number of postcards and greetings cards worked in pen and ink with washes of colour and heightened with touches of gold. Her illustrations, again like Jessie's, were mysterious and romantic with parallel titles such as 'The Enchanted Lodge' and 'The Queen and the Gypsies'. Her figures were more substantial than Jessie's, closer to those of Burne-Jones than of 'The Four'. Annie French's characters had weight and were actors moving in some Celtic fairy tale. Jessie M. King's were fragile and belonged to her own personal dreams. Annie French had a rich sense of colour. She used dark or tinted backgrounds as a foil and illuminated her drawings with her own version of pointillism by scattering the picture with minute spots of primary colours and gold set against a fine reticulum of lines and dots that built up her dresses and landscapes. These were the equivalents of Jessie M. King's showers of petals but whereas, for all its decorativeness, Jessie's was linear work, Annie French's

176
Annie French, 'Fairy
Abundance', circa 192?.
Pen, ink and watercolour.
26 cm. × 37.5 cm. Private
collection.

was an arrangement of shapes. Nevertheless, it fulfilled the terms of the fairy-like themes with as much validity as Jessie's own.

Katherine Cameron (1874–1965), who was a product of the Glasgow School of Art and Cecile Walton 1891–1956), who studied at the Edinburgh College of Art, both worked mainly in watercolour in a more realist style. Katherine Cameron related to the Pre-Raphaelites in her figure drawing but one could see vestiges of the Glasgow Style in her contrived settings of an Art Nouveau nature and in the incorporation of the titles within the borders of the works. Cecile Walton's figures were more hieratic, with a formalism that appeared to be derived from Piero della Francesca's paintings. She used a narrow range of pale colours that gave her characters a strange otherworldliness like those of the illustrator F. Caley Robinson so that, as with Jessie M. King's, one was left wondering what lay beyond the captured moment.

Both Katherine Cameron and Cecile Walton lacked some of the fantasy that had always been present in Jessie M. King's art, a fantasy that needed stylisation to realise itself. In the 1930s, certain illustrators: Joyce Mercer, Gladys Peto and Rie Cramer among them, simplified and elongated their figures in the way that Jessie M. King had done, using similar bold colours, but it is possible that the jazz age and the stridency of Art Deco were as much responsible for their individuality as Jessie M. King's influence. The point about Jessie M. King's art is that it was not an outcome of the history of art but of a formula. It was the exploration, however successfully, of a by-way. It was hermetic and it was finite. It did not have within itself the means of its renewal. By the time she left for Paris in 1909, Jessie had exhausted the possibilities of the Art Nouveau style. It had become clear that there was nothing new to say in that idiom. Fortunately she was able to find a new beginning in the colourwork of Bakst and in the discovery of the use of colour in batik. The gossamer drawings of her earlier years were almost at an end. It is for this reason that she had no disciples of consequence. It is better that her art was not copied. Wonder and magic exist only because they are exceptional. Too much familiarity takes away their awesomeness. Jessie M. King's dream-like fantasies, her immaculate sense of design and her superb technique place her in the forefront of those poetical artists who have the gift of conjuring up enchantment and, in doing so, enrich our lives.

Chronology
and
Checklist

Chronology

1834   James Waters King born, Stirlingshire.

1846   Mary Ann Anderson born, Lanark.

1854   Francis H. Newbery born, Devon.

1868   Charles Rennie Mackintosh born, Glasgow.

1869   James King and Mary Anderson marry.

1870   Revd King appointed to the diocese of New Kilpatrick.

1871   Birth of Eva King.

1872   Birth of Adah King.

1873   Birth of Peggy King.

1874   Ernest Archibald Taylor born, Greenock.

1875   Jessie Marion King born, Bearsden.

1876   Birth of Graham King.

1885   Francis H. Newbery appointed director of the Glasgow School of Art.

1892   Jessie M. King registers at Glasgow School of Art.

1894   Death of Graham King.

1896   Miss Cranston's first Tea Room opens, Buchanan Street, Glasgow.
Mary Ann King dies.
First part of new Glasgow School of Art designed by Charles Rennie Mackintosh.

1897   Jessie M. King awarded Queens Prize and Free Studentship Glasgow School of Art.

1898   Revd King dies.
Jessie M. King awarded silver medal at National Competition, South Kensington.

1899   Jessie M. King exhibits Venice Biennale.
Appointed Tutor in Book Decoration and Design, Glasgow School of Art.
Moves to 101 St. Vincent Street, Glasgow.
Receives first commission for book design from Globus Verlag, Berlin.
E. A. Taylor commences work as designer for Wylie and Lochhead.

1900   Death of Peggy King.

1902   Article in *The Studio*, 'Miss Jessie M. King and her Work', by Walter R. Watson.
Receives gold medal for book design, Turin International Exhibition of Modern Decorative Art.
Visits Germany and Italy.
Exhibits Budapest, Royal Scottish Academy, Glasgow Institute.

1904   Visits France.

1905   First one-man exhibition, Bruton Street Galleries, London.

1906   Appointed Tutor in Ceramic Decoration, Glasgow School of Art.

1907   Exhibition at Annan's Gallery, Glasgow.

1907	E. A. Taylor moves to Salford.
1908	Buys Greengate, Kirkcudbright.
	Designs costumes for the Scottish National Pageant
	E. A. Taylor and Jessie M. King marry.
1909	Birth of Merle Taylor.
	Second Exhibition at Annan's Gallery, Glasgow.
1910	E. A. Taylor appointed professor at Tutor Hart's Studios, Paris, and Paris Correspondent of *The Studio*.
	Moves to 16 rue de la Grande Chaumière, Paris.
1911	Establishment of The Shealing Atelier, Paris.
	First Arran summer school.
1912	Third exhibition at Annan's Gallery, Glasgow.
	Bridges of Paris published.
	Exhibits at Paris Salon.
1913	Designs nursery for Musée Galliera, Paris.
1915	Returns to Scotland to take up residence at Greengate, Kirkcudbright.
1919	Exhibits New York, Indianapolis.
1920	The Shealing Atelier finally closed.
1921	Wins first Lauder Award of Glasgow Society of Lady Artists.
1922	Begins pottery decoration in conjunction with David Methvens.
1927	First Lanarkshire school with murals by Jessie M. King and E. A. Taylor.
	Exhibits at Wishart Brown's Gallery, Glasgow.
1931	Joint exhibition with Helen Paxton Brown, 'Spring in Three Rooms', Glasgow.
1932	Designs Paul Jones Tea Rooms, Kirkcudbright.
1935	Exhibits at Pearson & Westergard's Gallery, Glasgow.
1936	Death of Eva King.
1938	Death of lifelong companion Mary McNab.
1944	Designs murals for Dalbeattie Youth Centre.
1945.	Organises pageant for V.E. Day, Kirkcudbright.
1949	Death of Adah King.
	Jessie M. King dies, Kirkcudbright.
1951	Death of E. A. Taylor, Kirkcudbright.
1971	Jessie M. King Commemorative Exhibition, Glasgow.
1985	Death of Merle Taylor.

Check-List of Books Decorated by Jessie M. King

A check-list is a prototype bibliography. A true bibliography of Jessie M. King's works will probably never be completed because of certain insurmountable obstacles. Some of the gaps in my own list, compiled over some thirty years, have been filled in by Robin de Beaumont who generously allowed me access to his work notes. However, because of the closure of firms, the loss of records and the death of individuals, a number of facts are no longer available. Some relate to the dating of the hand-bindings that Jessie M. King designed when she was a pupil and instructor at the Glasgow School of Art. Other problems arise in connection with the many variant bindings for the Foulis books and for the *Spenser* and *Shelley* volumes of 1906/7. These might well be sorted out in time if records, presumed lost, come to light again. The main obstacle, though, relates to the covers that Jessie King did around 1903 for Routledge.

Jessie M. King designed twenty-four sets of lettering and three different cover pictures for one of Routledge's series of children's classics. These were reprints of editions that had been on Routledge's list for many years. Each volume had originally contained approximately six chromolithographic illustrations by various artists. The new edition contained only four of these illustrations, and the choice varied from printing to printing. Routledge used no fewer than six printing firms. Each title was available in covers of blue, red or green cloth. Each colour could have any one of Jessie M. King's three designs: a fairy child, a young girl or an older girl. Each one of these could have any four of the six chromolithographic illustrations. If, as does not seem unlikely, all these permutations exist, the total number of possibilities for each title is 270. Any bibliophile who wishes to collect every combination of each of the twenty-four titles needs considerable shelf space, a long and active life and a healthy bank balance.

This check-list includes every book that I am aware of to have original art work by Jessie M. King, whether in the form of illustrations, cover designs, endpapers, title-pages, head- or tail-pieces or other ornaments. It also includes booklets, such as *Whose Land?*, which contain several illustrations by Jessie M. King and which deserve bibliographical mention. No doubt more titles and variants will be found which will make amendments necessary and confirm that this, like other check-lists, should be regarded as 'work-in-progress'.

The list is divided as follows:
A Unique copies designed, illustrated and bound by or for Jessie M. King.
B Books decorated/illustrated by Jessie M. King.
C Books with reproductions of work by Jessie M. King not commissioned expressly for the volume and not reproduced elsewhere.
D Books containing textual material by Jessie M. King other than in A, B, C above.
E A short list of printed ephemera.

A *Unique copies*
1 Dante Gabriel Rossetti, *Ballads* (Siddall Edition), pub. Ellis & Elvey 1899, bound Chivers, Bath, c. 1900, limp vellum with upper and lower cover drawing and spine lettering in pen, ink and gilt by Jessie M. King, $6\frac{1}{2}$ in. × $4\frac{3}{4}$ in.

2 Emile Zola, *Le Rêve* pub. Marpon & Flammerion, Paris, 1892, bound green morocco by John Macbeth, Glasgow, c. 1900, gold tooled design on upper and lower covers and spine by Jessie M. King, sgd; frontispiece in pen, ink on vellum by Jessie M. King, sgd, made up of a series of weekly parts illus. Carloz Schwabe, 335 + ix pp., $11\frac{1}{2}$ in. × $7\frac{1}{2}$ in.

3 *Poems by Christina Rossetti*, ? Macmillan, 1891, coarse-grain morocco, bound MacLehose & Sons, Glasgow, c. 1900, gold tooling on upper cover and spine by Jessie M. King.

4 Catulle Mendes (trans.), *L'Evangile de L'Enfance de Notre Seigneur Jesus Christ Selon Saint Pierre*, pub. Armand Colin, Paris 1894, vellum, bound MacLehose & Sons, c. 1900. 14 full page col. plates and 97 pict. borders by Carloz Schwabe, design and lettering in gilt on covers and spine by Jessie M. King, frontispiece in pen, ink on vellum by Jessie M. King, 185 pp., 13 in. × $9\frac{1}{4}$ in.

5 Thomas Lodge, *The Story of Rosalynde*, pub. Newnes (Caxton Series), 1902, one of 30 copies on japon sgd by Edmund J. Sullivan, 10 b/w illustrations by Edmund J. Sullivan. Vellucent binding by Chivers, Bath, with design on covers and spine in pen, ink stained with red, lilac green and gold with mother-of-pearl inlay by Jessie M. King, 8vo, 187 pp. A second copy of this exists with a slightly modified design in the Museum of Binding, Bath.

6 *The Rubáiyát of Omar Khayyám*, edition unknown, levant morocco, bound MacLehose & Sons, Exhibited Scottish National Exhibition, 1911.

7 W. M. Thackeray, *The Rose and the Ring*, bound John Macbeth? Exhibited Scottish National Exhibition, 1911.

8 Michael Farless, *The Road Mender*, pub. Duckworth & Co, 1902, bound green morocco by John Macbeth?, c. 1905, gilt design on upper cover and lettering on spine by Jessie M. King, viii + 158 pp., 6½ in. × 4½ in. Exhibited Scottish Arts Council Exhibition, 1971, Lot 102 at Glasgow sale, 1977. Inscribed 'O Nameless One! I.L.Y.V.M.'

9 Tennyson, *Poems*, edition unknown, bound vellum, MacLehose & Sons, c. 1905. Exhibited Scottish National Exhibition, 1911.
Another volume of Tennyson's works bound by MacLehose in blue morocco, possibly to Jessie M. King's design, was also exhibited.

10 *The High History of the Holy Graal*, pub. Dent/Dutton, 1903, Vellucent binding by Chivers, Bath, with pen, ink, watercolour design on upper cover by Jessie M. King, xvii + 380 pp., 9 in. × 5¾ in., 1/225 large paper copies. *See B 21.*

B *Books Decorated by Jessie M. King*
(c) = cover design; (ep) = endpaper(s); (p) = preliminaries; (ht) = half-title; (t) = title-page; (hp) = headpiece; (tp) = tailpiece, (fp) = frontispiece; (cn) = colophon. Other abbreviations correspond to common usage. In some cases the title on the spine is an abbreviated version of the title on the cover. In the check-list the cover title is always used. All measurements are in inches.
  1 *Album Von Berlin*, Globus Verlag, Berlin, (1899), (c)
        i Abstract design in blue, green, black and gold on cream paper bds. sgd, three double-page plus 49 single-page photographs, 10¾ in. × 13½ in.
        ii Design with central female figure, sgd, dated 1899.
        iii As (i) but with contents expanded to include the Western Suburbs and Potsdam, 1902.
        iv Reprints of (i) with differing nos. of plates mentioned on title page, 1902, 1903, 1905.
        v Smaller version of (i) (?1907) (1904, de Beaumont), 3 double-page plus 45 plates, 6 in. × 7¾ in.

2 *Album Von Dresden und Sachische Schweitz*, Globus Verlag, Berlin, (1899), (c), sgd, stylised figure design in white, red and green on grey paper bds, 10¾ in. × 13½ in.

3 Anna Schober, *Hanna*, Globus Verlag, Berlin, (1899), (c), pale blue, dark blue and gold design on cloth, photographic fp after Paul Heyder, 180 pp., 8 in. × 5½ in.

4 *Album Von Frankfurt Am Main*, Globus Verlag, Berlin, (1899), (c). Same cover design as Album von Berlin (ii) with new titling in panel, sgd, dated 1899, 23 photographic plates, 10¾ in. × 13½ in.

5 *Die Denkmaler Der Siegesallee*, Globus Verlag, Berlin, (1899), (c). Same cover design as Album von Berlin (i) with new lettering not by JMK, sgd, 3 double-page + 37 single-page photographic plates of the monuments in the Berlin Sieges Allee.

6 *Rund Um Berlin*, Globus Verlag, Berlin, (1899), (c), abstract design in blue, pink, lemon and green on grey paper bds, sgd, 10¾ in. × 13½ in.

7 *A View of Edinburgh and District*, Patrick Thomson Cash Drapery Stores, Edinburgh, (?1900), (c), sgd, dated 1899.
Same cover and design as 1(ii) above. Possibly printed by Globus, Berlin, in association with Wertheim's and Thomson's stores.

8 (George G. Napier), *The Burial of Lady John Scott, Authoress of 'Annie Laurie'*, a poem privately printed by MacLehose & Sons, 1900, blue/green paper wrappers with mtd label on upper and lower covers not by JMK, one etching by Muirhead Bone, one dec. page by D. Y. Cameron, one dec. page by JMK, 12 pp., 9 in. × 6 in.

9 Lord Tennyson, *Early Poems*, David Bryce & Son, Glasgow, Frederick A. Stokes Co, New York (1900), (Bryce's Dainty Little Library no. 1), (c) leather, gilt, (t), 3½ in. × 2¼ in.

10 Lord Tennyson, *English Idylls*, David Bryce & Son, Glasgow, Frederick A. Stokes Co, New York (1900), (Bryce's Dainty Little Library no. 2), (c) leather, gilt, (t), (as 9), 3½ in. × 2¼ in.

11 Lord Tennyson, *The Princess*, David Bryce & Son, Glasgow, Frederick A. Stokes Co, New York (1900), (Bryce's Dainty Little Library no. 3), (c) leather, gilt, (t), (as 9), 3½ in. × 2¼ in.

12 Lord Tennyson, *In Memoriam*, David Bryce & Son, Glasgow, Frederick A. Stokes Co, New York (1900), (Bryce's Dainty Little Library,

no. 4), (c) leather, gilt, (t), (*as 9*), $3\frac{1}{2}$ in. × $2\frac{1}{4}$ in.

13 Lord Tennyson, *Maud*, David Bryce & Son, Glasgow, Frederick A. Stokes Co, New York (1900), (Bryce's Dainty Little Library no. 5), (c) leather, gilt, (t), (*as 9*), $3\frac{1}{2}$ in. × $2\frac{1}{4}$ in.

14 Lord Tennyson, *Tennyson's Poems*, David Bryce & Son, Glasgow, Frederick A. Stokes Co, New York (?1900), (Bryce's Dainty Little Library) (c) green leather, gilt, (t) and repeated on rear free endpaper, (*as 9*). A compendium of 9–13 above printed on India Paper, 960 pp., $3\frac{1}{4}$ in. × $2\frac{1}{4}$ in.

15 Sir Walter Scott, *Lady of the Lake*, David Bryce & Son, Glasgow, Frederick A. Stokes Co, New York (1900), (Bryce's Dainty Little Library no. 6), (c) leather, gilt, (t), (*as 9*), $3\frac{1}{2}$ in. × $2\frac{1}{4}$ in.

16 Sir Walter Scott, *Lord of the Isles*, David Bryce & Son, Glasgow, Frederick A. Stokes Co, New York (1900), (Bryce's Dainty Little Library no. 7), (c) leather, gilt, (t), (*as 9*), $3\frac{1}{2}$ in. × $2\frac{1}{4}$ in.

17 Robert Burns, *Songs*, David Bryce & Son, Glasgow, Frederick A. Stokes Co, New York (1900), (Bryce's Dainty Little Library no. 8), (c) leather, gilt, (t), (*as 9*), $3\frac{1}{2}$ in. × $2\frac{1}{4}$ in.

18 Robert Burns, *Poems*, David Bryce & Son, Glasgow, Frederick A. Stokes Co, New York (1900), (Bryce's Dainty Little Library no. 9), (c) leather, gilt, (t), (*as 9*), $3\frac{1}{2}$ in. × $2\frac{1}{4}$ in.

19 *Gleanings from Wordsworth*, David Bryce & Son, Glasgow, Frederick A. Stokes Co, New York (1900), (Bryce's Dainty Little Library no. 10), (c) leather, gilt, (t), (*as 9*), $3\frac{1}{2}$ in. × $2\frac{1}{4}$ in.

20 Thomas Moore, *Irish Melodies*, David Bryce & Son, Glasgow, Frederick A. Stokes Co, New York (1900), (Bryce's Dainty Little Library no. 11), (c) green leather, gilt, (t), (*as 9*), 128 pp., $3\frac{1}{2}$ in. × $2\frac{1}{4}$ in. (upper cover has title *Moore's Poems*).

21 Lord Macaulay, *Lays of Ancient Rome*, David Bryce & Son, Glasgow, Frederick A. Stokes Co, New York (1900), (Bryce's Dainty Little Library no. 12), (c) green leather, gilt, (t), (*as 9*), $3\frac{1}{2}$ in. × $2\frac{1}{4}$ in.

22 Oliver Goldsmith, *She Stoops to Conquer*, David Bryce & Son, Glasgow, Frederick A. Stokes Co, New York (?1901), (Bryce's Dainty Little Library no. 13), (c) leather, gilt, (t), (*as 9*), $3\frac{1}{2}$ in. × $2\frac{1}{4}$ in.

23 Oliver Goldsmith, *(The) Deserted Village*, David Bryce & Son, Glasgow, Frederick A.

Stokes Co, New York (?1901), (Bryce's Dainty Little Library no. 14), (c) leather, gilt, (t), (*as 9*), $3\frac{1}{2}$ in. × $2\frac{1}{4}$ in.

24 *Neuer Deutscher Novellenschatz* no. 14 (of 23 issued volumes), ed. Paul Heyse and Ludwig Lastner, containing three stories:
(a) Ein Doppeleben by Joseph Victor Widmann
(b) Eine Schwartze Kugel by A. Godin
(c) Die Danidae by Ernest von Wildenbruch Globus Verlag, Berlin (1902), (c), upper and lower cover and spine in green, pink and blue on grey cloth, 236 pp., $7\frac{1}{4}$ in. × $4\frac{3}{4}$ in. Lower cover sgd, JMK. dec. ep poss not by JMK.

25 *Werke Alter Meister*, No. 1, *Konigl Museum Berlin*, Globus Verlag, Berlin (1902), (c), (ep), (t), buckram cover with figure, birds, foliage, sgd, dated 1902, $13\frac{1}{2}$ in. × 11 in.

26 *Musik und Gesang*, Globus Verlag, Berlin (1902), (c), (ep), (t). Upper and lower covers and spine in black on grey-green cloth, figure design, grey-white pict. ep with fairy design, $13\frac{1}{2}$ in. × $10\frac{1}{2}$ in.

27 George Buchanan, *Jephtha*, trans. from the Latin by A. Gordon Mitchell, pub. Alex Gardner, Paisley (1902), (c), green dec. cloth, gilt, (t), 4 b/w illus, (tp), 130 pp., 8 in. × $5\frac{1}{4}$ in.

28 *The Mabinogion*, trans. Lady Charlotte Guest, Dent 1903, (Temple Classics), b/w fp, used again in *The High History of the Holy Graal* (B35) under a different title, blue cloth gilt, 360 pp., $6\frac{1}{4}$ in. × 4 in. Also leather.

29 Lord Tennyson, *The Morte D'Arthur*, Routledge 1903 (Nov.), (The Broadway Booklets), green card cover not by JMK, b/w fp, and 3 b/w illus. by JMK, 28 pp., $5\frac{3}{4}$ in. × $4\frac{3}{4}$ in. Also suede.

30 Lord Tennyson, *Guinevere*, Routledge 1903 (Nov.), (The Broadway Booklets), green card cover not by JMK, halftone fp and three b/w illus. by JMK, 42 pp., $5\frac{3}{4}$ in. × $4\frac{3}{4}$ in. Also suede.

31 Lord Tennyson, *Elaine*, Routledge 1903 (Nov.), (The Broadway Booklets), terracotta card cover not by JMK, b/w fp, and 3 b/w illus. by JMK, 80 pp., $5\frac{3}{4}$ in. × $4\frac{3}{4}$ in. Also issued 1905 green cloth, gilt. Nos. 29, 30, 31 also issued as three poems in one volume. Also suede.

32 *Rubáiyát of Omar Khayyám* trans. Edward Fitzgerald, Routledge 1903, (The Broadway Booklets), red card cover not by JMK, b/w fp,

and 3 b/w illus. by JMK, 48 pp., $5\frac{3}{4}$ in. × $4\frac{3}{4}$ in.
Also blue calf gilt, green suede gilt, tan calf,
red cloth gilt, green cloth gilt.
Also pub. Boots Ltd, (Farrington Booklets),
nd, light brown calf gilt.

33 Mrs M. W. Spielmann, *Littledom Castle and
Other Tales*, Routledge 1903 (Oct.), one b/w
illus. 'The Magic Garret' by JMK, col. fp. and
illus. by Hugh Thomson and others, purple
dec. cloth gilt not by JMK, x + 337 pp.,
$7\frac{1}{2}$ in. × $5\frac{1}{2}$ in.
Also red cloth gilt.

34 Charles Kingsley, *The Heroes*, Routledge 1903
(Nov.), (Playmate Series), dec. (t) and four b/w
illus. by JMK, green cloth gilt, 147 pp.,
$7\frac{1}{2}$ in. × $4\frac{1}{2}$ in.
Also red cloth gilt.
Also blue cloth gilt.

35 *The Holy Graal* (cover and spine titled thus) =
The High History of the Holy Graal, trans.
Sebastian Evans, Dent/Dutton 1903 (Oct.), (c)
pale blue black pict. cloth gilt, pict. (ht), pict.
(t), 22 b/w illus. (some with red borders), 36
(hp), xvii + 380 pp., 9 in. × $5\frac{3}{4}$ in.
Also brown morocco gilt.
Also de-luxe ltd edn, 250 copies on large paper,
vellum, pict. blue gilt with (t) and the 22 illus.
on India paper.
Also see A 10.
Also see B 28.

36 William Morris, *The Defence of Guinevere and
Other Poems*, John Lane 1903 (Nov.) but dated
1904, (c) red cloth with gilt designs
on upper and lower cover and spine by JMK,
b/w dec. (ht), dec. (fp), (t) and 65 b/w decs of
which 24 are full page, 310 pp., $7\frac{3}{4}$ in. × $5\frac{1}{4}$ in.

37 *The Life of Saint Mary Magdalen*, trans.
Valentina Hawtrey, John Lane 1903 (Oct.) but
dated 1904, (c) green cloth with
gilt dec. on upper and lower cover and spine
by JMK, illus. with photographs, xxii +
285 pp., $7\frac{1}{2}$ in. × $5\frac{1}{4}$ in.

38 Dean Swift, *Gulliver's Travels*, Routledge
(March 1903), (3s 6d Prize Series) (c), pict.
design in gilt and white on coloured cloth by
JMK, 3 col. pl. + 43 b/w illus. by E. J. Wheeler,
xvi + 414 pp., 8 in. × $5\frac{1}{4}$ in.
See introduction to this check-list. To add still
further to the confusion, some of the 'fairy
child' covers have a single gold swallow on the
spine below the title. Later editions were also
issued in conjunction with Dutton of New
York so that a variant of the title-page exists.

Other variant title-pages exist with 'Broadway
House' rather than 'Broadway, Ludgate Hill'
at the foot.

39 John B. Marsh, *The Life and Adventures of
Robin Hood*, Routledge (1903) as above, 19
illus. (publisher's catalogue calls for 20) by
Gordon Browne + 4 cp, 8 in. × $5\frac{1}{4}$ in.

40 Revd. J. G. Wood, *The Boy's Own Book of
Natural History*, Routledge 1903 (dated 1901
on title-page), as above, 2 col. pl. + 330 b/w
illus. by unnamed artists, vi + 378 pp.,
8 in. × $5\frac{1}{4}$ in.

41 John Bunyan, *The Pilgrim's Progress*,
Routledge (March 1903), as above, 4 col. pl. +
54 b/w illus. by J. D. Watson, 448 pp.,
8 in. × $5\frac{1}{4}$ in.

42 Hans Andersen *Fairy Tales and Stories*,
Routledge (March 1903), as above, 4 col. pl. +
60 b/w illus. by A. W. Bayes, vii + 512 pp.,
8 in. × $5\frac{1}{2}$ in.

43 *Grimms Fairy Tales*, Routledge (1903), as
above, 4 col. pl. by Nister + b/w illus. title-
page + 12 b/w illus. by E. H. Weinhert, 512 pp.,
$7\frac{3}{4}$ in. × $5\frac{1}{4}$ in.

44 *The Arabian Nights' Entertainments*,
Routledge 1904, as above, 4 col. pl. by A. W.
Cooper, vii + 501 + ii pp., 8 in. × $5\frac{1}{2}$ in.

45 Daniel Defoe, *Robinson Crusoe*, Routledge
1904, as above, 4 col. pl. + 52 b/w illus. by
J. D. Watson, xxvi + 566 + x pp., 8 in. × $5\frac{1}{4}$ in.

46 J. D. Wyss, *The Swiss Family Robinson*, ed.
W. H. G. Kingston, Routledge 1904 as above,
4 col. pl. + ?95 b/w illus., 564 pp., 8 in. × $5\frac{1}{4}$ in.

47 Thomas Day, *Sandford and Merton*, ed.
Belinda Blinders, Routledge (?1904), as above,
4 (? = 8) col. pl. + 60 b/w illus., 448 pp.,
8 in. × $5\frac{1}{4}$ in.

48 Maria Edgeworth, *Early Lessons*, Routledge
(?1904), as above, 1 col. pl. + 24 b/w illus. by
F. A. Fraser in each of the three stories in the
book, 185 + ii + 188 + ii + 180 pp., 8 in. × $5\frac{1}{4}$ in.

49 Charles Dickens, *A Child's History of England*,
Routledge (?1904), as above, 8 col. pl. by
unnamed artist (?Sir John Gilbert), viii +
344 pp., 8 in. × $5\frac{1}{4}$ in.

50 Revd. J. H. Ingraham, *Prince of the House of
David*, Routledge (?1904), as above, 1 col.
pl. + 12 b/w, 426 pp., 8 in. × $5\frac{1}{4}$ in.

51 Gilbert White, *A Natural History of Selborne*,

Routledge (1904), as above, ?6 col. pl. + b/w by Harrison Weir, 475 pp., 8 in. × 5¼ in.

52 Charles Lamb, *Lamb's Tales from Shakespeare*, Routledge (Nov. 1904), as above, 4 col. pl. by Sir John Gilbert, viii + 405 pp., 7¾ in. × 5¼ in.

53 Revd. J. G. Wood, *Wood's Illustrated Natural History*, Routledge (?1904), as above, 2 col. pl. + 480 b/w illus. by William Harvey, x + 444 pp., 8 in. × 5¼ in. The unexpurgated version of B 40.

54 *Captain Cook's Voyages*, ed. Lt. Charles R. Low, Routledge (?1904), as above, 4 col. pl. + 28 b/w illus. by Gordon Browne and others, 512 pp., 8 in. × 5¼ in.
This volume demonstrates the difficulties encountered. The publisher's catalogue calls for 12 coloured plates. Each volume contains 4 of these. If the printers made their selections even-handedly there exist 495 different permutations of the plates alone!

55 Elizabeth Wetherell, *Queechy*, Routledge (?1904), as above, 4 col. pl. by Dorothy Foulger, 642 pp., 7¾ in. × 5¼ in.

56 Cervantes, *Don Quixote*, Routledge (?1904), as above, 4 col. pl. + 205 b/w illus. by Sir John Gilbert, x + 503 pp., 7¾ in. × 5¼ in.

57 *Aesop's Fables*, trans. Revd. G. F. Townsend, Routledge (?1904), as above, 4 col. pl. + 114 illus. by Harrison Weir, 256 pp., 8 in. × 5¼ in.

58 Captain Marryat, *Children of the New Forest*, Routledge (?1904), as above, 8 col. pl. by Sir John Gilbert + 54 b/w illus. by Paul Hardy, v + 409 pp., 8 in. × 5 in.

59 Tennyson's Poems, Routledge (?1902), as above, vi + 613 bp 8 in × 5¼ in

60–61 These refer to the remaining two volumes in the Routledge series above. The firm published four other volumes in the 3s. 6d Prize Series: *Uncle Tom's Cabin, Mother Goose's Nursery Rhymes, Edgeworth's Parents' Assistant, Edgeworth's Popular Tales*. Two of these, so far unlocated, will have cover designs by JMK.

62 William Morris, *The Defence of Guinevere*, John Lane (Oct. 1904), (Flowers of Parnassus Series no. 22—of 27 nos.), dk. green pict. cl. gilt, (c), (ht), (t), 7 b/w illus., 5 pages decs., 43 pp., 5¾ in. × 4½ in.
Also green morocco gilt.
Also reprinted Scolar Press (1979), green/grey cloth gilt, also suede gilt, also 12 unnumbered copies on beige silk gilt, 46 pp., 6¾ in. × 4¾ in.

63 *Schmuck und Edelmetallarbeiten*, Alexander Koch, Darmstadt (1904), (Koch's Monographien IX), (t), white pict. cloth gilt by Fritz Scholl, (t) by JMK.

64 Milton, *Comus*, Routledge (Photogravure and Colour Series), (Nov. 1905), dated 1906, (c) red/green dec. cloth gilt, (fp), (t), (p), 9 photogravure illus., 84 pp., 8½ in. × 5¾ in.
Also black quarter cloth beige bds. with same lettering on spine.
Also suede, yapp edges, gilt.

65 *The Poems of Spenser*, ed. W. B. Yeats, T.C. & E.C. Jack (The Golden Poets Series), (Oct. 1906), tinted fp and title by A. S. Hartrick, 8 illus. in b/w, red, gold, sgd by JMK, lvii + 290 pp., 6¾ in. × 4½ in., dec. blue cloth gilt with 'Illustrated by Jessie M. King' on spine.
Also mottled green cloth gilt.
Also dec. brown cloth gilt.
Also green leather with grille pattern in blind and gilt lettering.
Also under the imprint of The Caxton Press in dec. brown cloth gilt. Ibid, in blue cloth gilt. Ibid, in morocco backed cloth, spine gilt. Ibid, in quarter green calf.

66 *Budding Life*, An Album of Drawings by Jessie M. King, Gowans & Gray, (Nov. 1906), pict. parchment wrappers (ht), (t), 14 b/w drawings, 32 unnumbered pp., 8½ in. × 5½ in.
Reprinted Dec. 1906, Nov. 1907.
Also de-luxe edition, 1907, silver-grey wrappers with new design, 10¼ in. × 7¾ in.

67 S. T. Coleridge, *Ancient Mariner*, Foulis Press (Roses of Parnassus Series no. 11), (1906?) (BL Cat. suggests 1903 but this is not possible stylistically), upper and lower pict. wrappers by JMK, (t), (hp), and 6 tp not by JMK, iv + 38 + ii pp., 7 in. × 3½ in.

68 *Our Trees and How to Know Them*, Gowans & Gray (Nature Books no. 8), 1906 (July), parchment wrappers by JMK, 60 b/w photographs by Charles Kirk, viii + 68 + iv pp., 6 in. × 4 in.
Reprinted December 1906, September 1907, April 1908, August 1911, June 1916.

69 Jeremy Taylor, *The Marriage Ring*, Gowans & Gray (International Library no. 3), 1906, col. parchment wrappers by JMK, 49 pp., 6 in. × 4 in.

70 *Everyman, a Morality Play*, Gowans & Gray (International Library no. 6), (Oct. 1906), col. parchment wrappers by JMK, 52 pp., 6 in. × 4 in.

Also Nov. 1907, also March 1921, also March 1930, Thomas Nelson & Son.

71 Christina Rossetti, *Goblin Market and Other Poems*, Gowans & Gray (International Library no. 7), March 1907, col. parchment wrappers by JMK, xi + 99 pp., 6 in. × 4 in.
Also March 1914.

72 Maurice Maeterlinck, *Alladine and Palomides*, Gowans & Gray (International Library no. 11), Sept. 1907, col. parchment wrappers by JMK, 56 + viii pp., 6in. × 4in.
Also 1911.

73 Lady Alix Egerton, *The Masque of the Two Strangers*, Gowans & Gray, Nov. 1907, col. parchment wrappers by JMK, 32 pp., 6 in. × 4 in.
Also 1926.

74 *The Poems of Shelley*, Selected with an Introduction by Prof. J. Churton Collins, T.C. & E.C. Jack (The Golden Poets Series), (Sept. 1907), tinted photogravure fp and (t) by A. S. Hartrick, 8 illus. in b/w, red, gold by JMK, sgd, xlvi + 246 pp., 6¾ in. × 4½ in., dark blue/purple cloth with gilt design of horizontal straps.
Also plain blue cloth.
Also under the imprint of The Caxton Press in dec. brown cloth gilt, uniform with 51 above.
Ditto in dec. blue cloth gilt with dec. harp design.
Ditto in red cloth with dec. harp design in white and gilt, fractionally larger in size.

75 Keats, *Isabella, or the Pot of Basil*, T. N. Foulis (Envelope Books no. 3), Nov. 1907, mounted col. (fp), col. pict. (t), b/w (hp), 3 col. pl. sgd, 42 pp., 6½ in. × 3½ in., grey paper wrappers with design on upper, lower covers and spine, plates not tipped in, outer 'Envelope Book' wrapper.
Also green cloth, gilt on spine.
Also brown suede.
Also blue calf yapp blind. Also red calf yapp blind.
Also velvet yapp gilt with tipped-in plates.
Also paper wrappers with pict. onlay of a portion of one of the plates in different col. scheme, tipped-in plates.
Also grey cloth bds with design in green, dk grey, gilt, tipped-in plates, 7¼ in. × 3½ in.

76 Maurice Maeterlinck, *Interior*, trans. William Archer, Gowans & Gray (International Library no. 20), May 1908, col. parcht wrappers by JMK, 31 pp., 6 in. × 5 in.
Also 1911.

77 *Nature Pictures*, Gowans & Gray, twelve-part fortnightly periodical beginning 23 July 1908, terracotta wrappers by JMK, 30–40 photographs in each part, 12½in. × 9¾in.
Also bound complete in red cloth with same design in black and gilt, 192 pp.
Also 1912 ? olive-green cloth.
Also in French as *Tableaux de la Nature*, Perche, Paris, July 1908, (c) as before red cloth gilt.
Also brown cloth with design in black.
Also 1912 in olive-green cloth.

78 Paolo Montegazza, *The Legends of Flowers* (First Series), T. N. Foulis (1908), col. (fp) by Walter Crane, dec. borders to each page by JMK, 152 pp., 7½ in. × 4¾ in., white cloth gilt with design by JMK.

79 *Aucassin and Nicolette*, trans. F. W. Bourdillon, T. N. Foulis (Envelope Books no. 5), (Nov. 1908), 4 col. pl. by Katherine Cameron, col. paper wrappers by JMK, 67 pp., 6¾ in. × 3¼ in.
Also grey-brown yapp suede.
Also leather.
Also 1913 as 'Foulis Friendship Booklets no. 4' with col. (fp), col. (t), plus 2 col. pl. by Katherine Cameron, col. pict. wrappers by JMK, 68 + ii pp.
Ditto in silk with marker, ? trans. W. E. Sparkes, see no. 98.

80 Maurice Maeterlinck, *The Seven Princesses*, trans. William Metcalf, Gowans & Gray (International Library no. 28), June 1909, col. parcht. wrappers by JMK, 48 pp., 5¾ in. × 5 in.
Also 1911.

81 Maurice Maeterlinck, *The Death of Tintagles*, trans. Alfred Dutro, Gowans & Gray (International Library no. 26), June 1909, col. parcht wrappers by JMK, 44 pp., 5¾ in. × 5 in.
Also 1911.

82 *Our Flowering Shrubs and How to Know Them*, Gowans & Gray (Gowans Nature Books no. 23), 1909, 60 photographic reproductions after Charles Kirk, col. parcht wrappers by JMK, viii + 72 pp., 5¾ in. × 5 in.
Also 1916, 1918.

83 Paolo Mantegazza, *The Legends of Flowers* (Second Series), T. N. Foulis, 1909, col. (fp) by Walter Crane, pict. borders to each page by JMK, identical to 62, white cloth gilt with pict. onlay by Rodin, x + 168 pp., 7½ in. × 4¾ in.

84 J. H. Crawford, *The Wild Flowers*, T. N.

Foulis, 1909 16 col. pl. by Edwin Alexander, text by John Williamson, brown buckram with gold design on front by JMK, 232 pp., ?6¼ in. × 5½ in.
Also 2nd edn, 1909.
Also as *Les Fleurs Sauvages Chez Elles*, Première Serie and Seconde Serie (2 vols), Perch, Paris?(c) by JMK.
Also as *Wild Wachsende Blume zu Hause*, (2 vols), Wilhelm Weicher, Leipzig, ?(c) by JMK.

85 *Poems of Ralph Waldo Emerson*, Dodge Publishing Co, New York (The Choice Books), nd (?1909) cream japon bds with col japon onlays in relief on upper cover and spine by JMK, sgd, 231 pp., 5¾ in. × 4 in.

86 *Dwellings of an Old World Town: A Book of Drawings in Black and White by Jessie M. King*, Gowans & Gray, 1909 (Dec.), pict. (t), plus 24 b/w illus. by JMK, col. pict. wrappers by JMK, 51 pp., 8¾ in. × 5¾ in.
Also parch gilt.
Also 1909 variant with (t) caption 'London & Glasgow, 1909, Gowans and Gray Ltd, published by T. N. Foulis, Edinburgh and London'.
Also with same cover design as 1909 but with the addition of 'Culross Fifeshire [sic]' and omitting the date '1909'.
Also boards with dust wrapper, b/w illus. and lettering on upper wrapper and extra outside wrapper with illus. on upper leaf by JMK for posting.

87 Paolo Mantegazza, *The Legends of Flowers* (Third Series), T. N. Foulis 1910, col (fp) by Walter Crane, dec. borders to each page by JMK identical to 62, white cloth gilt not by JMK, 155 pp., 7½ in. × 4¾ inc.

88 *The Grey City of the North*, T. N. Foulis (Cities Series no. 4), Nov. 1910 col. pict. wrappers by JMK, pict. contents page, pict. (t) + 24 b/w illus. by JMK, 51 pp., 8¼ in. × 5 in.
Also parch gilt.
Also 1912 paper wrappers with dec. upper and lower covers.
Also July 1914 omitting 'T. N. Foulis, Edinburgh & London' and substituting 'Edinburgh'.
Also off-white cloth bds.
Also July 1921 grey wrappers with mtd onlay ('The Queen's Post').
Also July 1925 new wrappers with illus. 'The Queen's Post at the Castle' and addition of words 'Edinburgh Drawings by Jessie M. King'.

Also Dec. 1984, Polygon Books with new foreword by Anne Barren Skipwith, stiff paper wrappers over bds with paler design of original cover illus.

89 *A Whip at the Mast*, ed. Revd. J. J. Mauley, James McKechnie & Sons, Greenock, (1911), col. pict. grey wrappers sgd by JMK, 64 pp., 7½ in. × 4½ in.

90 James Hogg, *Kilmeny*, T. N. Foulis (London Booklets no. 9), 1911 (Oct.). col. (fp), + 2 col. pl., by JMK, dec. paper wrappers with mtd col. pl. by JMK, 31 + ii pp., 6 in. × 3¼ in. (*See also 79.*)
Also brown suede, blind dec.
Also blue suede, blind dec.

91 *The City of the West*, T. N. Foulis (Cities Series no. 3), 1911, col. pict. wrappers, pict (t), mtd pict. contents page + 24 mtd b/w illus. by JMK, 27 pp., 8¼ in. × 5 in.
Also 1911 with different col. design on upper & lower covers and spine and new title *Glasgow: The City of the West*.
Also ditto without mtd plates.
Also Dec. 1984, Polygon Books with new foreword by Anne Barren Skipwith, stiff paper bds with the later cover design.

92 Edmé Arcambeau, *The Book of Bridges*, Gowans & Gray, 1911 (Dec.), col. (fp), + 17 col. pl. by JMK, green cloth gilt with mtd col. pl. by JMK limited to 1000 copies, 149 pp., 10¼ in. × 7½ in.
Also with French text as *Ponts de Paris* A. Perche, 1912, paper wrappers with revised col. cover picture.

93 James Hogg, *Songs and Poems of the Ettrick Shepherd*, T. N. Foulis (Songs of Life and Romance no. 3), (1912), pict. (t) and 6 col. pl. by JMK. The same illus. as *Kilmeny* (no. 76) enlarged, dec. blue cloth with mtd. col. pl. by JMK, iv + 152 + iv pp., 6¾ in. × 4½ in.
Also grey cloth gilt with mtd cp by JMK.
Also velvet persian, yapp edges.
Also cream paper wrappers, mtd col. pl. by JMK.

94 Robert Louis Stevenson, *Memories*, T. N. Foulis (Oct. 1912), col. pict. japon wrappers over card by JMK, 25 tipped-in b/w photographs, 56 pp., 8¼ in. × 5 in.
Also 'Boston Le Roy Phillips' added at foot of upper leaf of wrapper.
Also (1912) the design within borders and the above addition rubber stamped.
Also (1912) the design within borders without the addition.

Also the design within borders with the addition in type.
Also (Oct. 1914) dec. japon wrappers with new col. design by JMK. This now becomes no. 5 of the Cities Series replacing *Dwellings of an Old World Town*.
Also Oct. 1919 with the later design in orange, purple, green and grey.
Also ditto (1922).
Also ditto (1923).
Also ditto (1926).

95 R. W. Emerson, *Friendship*, T. N. Foulis (Foulis Friendship Booklets no. 1), (1913), col. japon wrappers by JMK, col. (fp) + col. (t) + 3 col. pl. by Preston Mcgoun, 42 + ii pp., $7\frac{1}{4}$ in. × $3\frac{3}{4}$ in.
Also silk with marker.

96 *Rubáiyát of Omar Khayyám*, T. N. Foulis (Foulis Friendship Books no. 2), (1913), col. upper & lower covers and spine by JMK, col. (fp), col. (t) + 2 col. pl. by Maurice Greiffenhagen, 39 + iv pp., $7\frac{1}{4}$ in. × $3\frac{1}{2}$ in.
Also with added imprint on (t) 'J. B. Lippincot Philadelphia also Boston Le Roy Phillips'.
Also silk with marker.

97 G. D. Rossetti (sic.), *The Blessed Damozel*, T. N. Foulis (Foulis Friendship Booklets no. 3), (1913), col. japon wrappers by JMK, col. (fp) + col. (t) + 2 col. pl. by Paul Wodroffe, 44 + ii pp., 7 in. × $3\frac{1}{2}$ in.
Also silk with marker.
Also embossed leather with design in blind.

98 *Aucassin and Nicolette* trans. F. W. Bourdillon, T. N. Foulis (Foulis Friendship Booklets no. 4), (1913), col. japon wrappers by JMK, col. (fp) + col. (t) + 2 col. pl. by Katherine Cameron, 68 + ii pp., $6\frac{3}{4}$ in. × $3\frac{1}{4}$ in.
Also silk with marker, see no. 79.

99 D. G. Rossetti, *Hand and Soul*, T. N. Foulis (Foulis Friendship Booklets no. 5), (1913), col. japon wrappers by JMK, col. (fp) + col. (t) + 2 col. pl. by William Hatherell, 41 pp., $7\frac{1}{4}$ in. × $3\frac{3}{4}$ in.

100 Robert Browning, *Rabbi Ben Ezra*, T. N. Foulis (Foulis Friendship Booklets no. 6), (1913), col. japon wrappers by JMK, col. (fp) + col. (t) + 2 col. pl. by Russell Flint, 40 + iv pp., $7\frac{1}{4}$ in. × $3\frac{1}{2}$ in.
Also limp suede with the JMK design in blind.
Also wrappers without the JMK design.
Also silk with marker.

101 *Christmas Carols*, T. N. Foulis (Foulis

Friendship Booklets no. 7), (1913), col. japon wrappers by JMK, col. (fp) + col. (t) + 2 col. pl. by William Hatherell, 38 + ii pp., 7 in. × $3\frac{3}{4}$ in.
Also silk with marker.
Also embossed leather.

102 Maurice Maeterlinck, *The Intruder*, Gowans & Gray, (International Library no. 43), 1913 (May), col. parcht wrappers by JMK, 50 + vi pp., 6 in. × 4 in.
Also 1914 (March).

103 Guy de Maupassant, *Three Tales by Maupassant*, retold by Lady Alix Egerton, Gowans & Gray, 1913, col. parcht wrappers by JMK, 36 pp., $5\frac{3}{4}$ in. × 5 in.

104 Cardinal Newman, *The Dream of Gerontius*, T. N. Foulis (Rose of Sharon Booklets no. 1), (1913), col. japon wrappers by JMK, col. pl. by R. T. Rose, 60 pp., 7 in. × $3\frac{1}{2}$ in.
Also larger format, wrappers without JMK design.

105 F. W. H. Myers, *St Paul*, T. N. Foulis (Rose of Sharon Booklets no. 2), (1913), col. japon wrappers by JMK, col. (fp), col. (t) + 2 col. pl. by W. Macdougal, 44 + ii pp., 7 in. × $3\frac{1}{2}$ in.
Also larger format, wrappers without JMK design, $7\frac{1}{2}$ in. × 4 in.

106 *The Poems of Lindsay Gordon*, T. N. Foulis (Foulis Open Air Booklets no. 1), (Oct. 1913), col. japon wrappers by JMK, 4 col. pl. by unnamed artist, 60 pp., $7\frac{1}{4}$ in. × $3\frac{1}{2}$ in.
Also Nov. 1919.

107 *The Lover of Gardens*, T. N. Foulis (Garden Lovers Booklet no. 1), (1913), col. japon wrappers by JMK, cp by Bearn & Parsons, 7 in. × $3\frac{1}{2}$ in.
Also velvet, yapp edges with same design in blind.

108 *The Spell of the Open Air*, T. N. Foulis (Foulis Open Air Booklets no. 2), (?1913), col. japon wrappers by JMK, col. (t) + 3 col. pl. by Harry Rountree, 43 + iii pp., $7\frac{1}{4}$ in. × $3\frac{1}{2}$ in.

109 *Seven Happy Days*, The Studio, Dec. 1913, 'A series of drawings by Jessie M. King with quotations from John Davidson and others', issued as a Christmas supplement in *The Studio*, 6 col. + 7 b/w illus. by JMK, 12 in. × $7\frac{3}{4}$ in.

110 *A Little Book of Sundial Mottoes*, T. N. Foulis (Garden Lovers Booklet no. 2), (1914), col. japon wrappers by JMK, 4 col. pl. by Alfred Rawlings, 38 pp., 7 in. × $3\frac{1}{2}$ in.
Also 1919, $7\frac{1}{4}$ in. × $3\frac{3}{4}$ in.

111 Launcelot Cross, *A Book of Sundials*, T. N.

Foulis (Foulis Grey Old Gardens Series), Oct. 1914, col. pict. paper bds by JMK, col. (fp) + 7 tipped-in col. pl. by Alfred Rawlings, 36 designs in verdigris by Warrington Hogg, x + 103 + ii pp., $7\frac{1}{2}$ in. × $5\frac{1}{4}$ in. Lettering in black on upper cover and spine label.
Also limp suede with impressed design.
Also April 1917 with lettering in black on upper cover and gilt on spine.
Also April 1917 with lettering in gilt on upper cover and spine. Tissue primary wrappers over bds, d/w with mtd col. pl. by Alfred Rawlings and lettering in grey in style of that on upper cover.
Also (Sept. 1922) all lettering black.

112 *Corners of Grey Old Gardens*, T. N. Foulis (Foulis Grey Old Gardens Series), 1914, pict. paper bds by JMK, 7 tipped-in col. pl. by Margaret Waterfield + 7 b/w (tp) by unnamed artist, vii + 151 pp., $7\frac{1}{2}$ in. × $5\frac{1}{2}$ in.
Lettering in black on upper cover and spine label.
Also lettering in gold on upper cover and spine, grey paper dust wrapper with mtd col. pl. by Margaret Waterfield, lettering by JMK.
Also (Sept. 1922), lettering in black on upper cover, gold on spine.
Also (Sept. 1922), lettering in black on upper cover, black on spine.
Also (1922) monochrome upper cover.

113 *Some Poems by Tom Pringle*, ed. J. M. Neale, T. N. Foulis (Foulis Open Air Booklets no. 3), (1916), col. japon wrappers by JMK, 4 col. pl. by Harry Rountree, 46 pp., $7\frac{1}{4}$ in. × $3\frac{1}{2}$ in.

114 Mrs Gaskell, *Cranford*, intr. by E. V. Lucas, Methuen (1914), pale green (ep) by JMK, b/w (fp) + dec. (t) + b/w illus. by Edmund H. New, dec. blue cloth gilt not by JMK, liii + 265 pp., 7 in. × $4\frac{1}{2}$ in.

115 Oscar Wilde, *A House of Pomegranates*, Methuen (1915), (ep) + col. (t) + 16 tipped-in col. pl. + 4 b/w dec. initial letters by JMK, pict. blue/yellow cloth by JMK, t.e.g., vi + 162 pp., $10\frac{1}{2}$ in. × $7\frac{1}{2}$ in.
Also American edition in red cloth.

116 Jessie M. King, *The Little White Town of Never Weary*, Harrap (Oct. 1917), col. (fp) + dec. (t) + 4 tipped-in col. pl. by JMK, 16 b/w photographs after JMK by J. Bruce Cameron, buff pict. cloth by JMK, 156 pp., 10 in. × $7\frac{3}{4}$ in.
Also specially bound, in batik box.

117 J. M. Neale, *A Carol: Good King Wenceslas*, *The Studio* (Nov. 1919), cream pict, wrappers + 12 col. pl. by JMK. Included inserted

slip advising that the drawings are for sale. Also pub. Leopold B. Hill, London (Sept. 1920), brown paper wrappers with mtd col. pict. labels of original upper and lower cover design, 12 tipped-in col. pl. by JMK, 26 unnumbered pp. + ii, $10\frac{1}{2}$ in. × $8\frac{3}{4}$ in.
Also (nd) by 'Macbeths of King Street who wish all their little friends a Merry Christmas'.
Also (nd) grey cloth with onlayed col. pl. by Eleanor Gorteswe Brickdale 32 pp.

118 Jessie Pope, *Whose Land?*, pub. Traffic Advertising Agency, London (1920), b/w (fp) + (t) + 6 full-page b/w illus. + 1 double-page b/w illus. + 6 dec. pages by JMK, cream paper wrappers with b/w illus. on upper and lower covers by JMK, 16 pp., $9\frac{1}{4}$ in. × $6\frac{1}{4}$ in.

119 Charles Lamb, *The Essays of Elia*, Methuen (1920), pale green (ep) by JMK (*as 114 above*) b/w
illus. by Garth Jones, blue cloth 254 pp., 7 in. × $4\frac{1}{4}$ in.

120 Rudyard Kipling, *L'Habitation Forcée*, trans. Louis Fabulet and Robert D'Humières, Kieffer, Paris, 1921, col. wrappers by JMK, dec. (t) + (ht) + 28 col. pl. in pochoir by JMK, bound by Kieffer in, variously, grey snakeskin, brown sealskin, lizard skin, all with embossed pict. gold onlay not by JMK, gilt, 96 + ii pp., $9\frac{1}{4}$ in. × 7 in. Limited to 500 copies on hand-made paper.
Also 50 copies on japon with an extra suite of the illus. in b/w.

121 *The Interlude of Youth*, intro. John Drinkwater, Gowans & Gray (Gowans International Library no. 46), (Aug. 1922), col. parcht wrappers by JMK, sgd, 39 pp., 6 in. × 5 in.
Also (1928).

122 Maud Cockerell, *Why the Fuchsia Hangs its Head*, Gowans & Gray, (Plays for Children no. 3), 1922 (Nov.), col. parcht wrappers by JMK, 6 in. × 5 in.

123 Harold Brighouse, *The Apple Tree*, Gowans & Gray (Repertory Plays no. 33), 1923, col. parcht wrappers by JMK, 37 pp., 6 in. × 4 in.

124 Jessie M. King, *How Cinderella was able to go to the Ball*, G. T. Foulis, London (Sept. 1924), col. pict. paper bds by JMK, tipped-in col. (fp) + tipped-in contents page + 8 tipped-in col. pl. by JMK, 4 single-page + 2 double-page tipped-in photographs after JMK, 55 pp., $8\frac{1}{4}$ in. × 6 in.
Also in batik bds in batik box by JMK.

Also black paper bds patterned yellow, white, red with white cloth spine, limited to 2000 copies.

125 *Hullo Boys*, Cecil Palmer, London, 1924, 2 col. pl. by JMK, pict. (ep) + (t) + 14 col. pics. + 57 photogravure text illus. by various artists, red pict. cloth gilt not by JMK, 160 pp., 10 in. × 7¼ in.

126 *Hullo Girls*, Cecil Palmer, 1924, same size, format and pagination as 125, 2 col. pl. by JMK, pict. (ep) + 14 col. pics. + 74 photogravure text illus. by various artists, blue pict. cloth gilt not by JMK.

127 *Hullo Boys*, Cecil Palmer, 1925, same size, format and cover dec. as 125, 1 illus. in verdigris by JMK, pict. (ep), dec. (t) + 12 col. pics. + 74 text illus. by various artists.

128 *Hullo Girls*, Cecil Palmer, 1925, same size, format and cover dec. as 126, 1 illus. in purple by JMK, pict. (ep), dec. (t), 12 col. pics. + 78 text illus. by various artists.

129 Maud Cockerell, *The Innkeeper's Shirt*, Gowans & Gray (Plays for Children no. 5), (1925), col. parcht wrappers by JMK, sgd, 35 pp., 6 in. × 5 in.

130 Lady Alix Egerton, *The Werewolf*, Gowans & Gray/Baker International Play Bureau, Boston, USA (Repertory Plays no. 50), 1926, col. parcht wrappers by JMK, 51 + ii pp., 6 in. × 4 in.

131 *Atalanta's Garland* (Book of the Edinburgh University Women's Union), Constable, 1926, 1 b/w illus., 'The Prince of the Fairies a-Wooing Came', by JMK, + b/w and col. illus. by Cecile Walton, Katherine Cameron and others, grey paper bds, 192 pp., 8¾ in. × 5½ in.
Also green cloth bds; also patterned terracotta bds, cream buckram spine.

132 Ida Gandy, *The Fairy Fruit*, Gowans & Gray (with over-label on tp. of Thomas Nelson) (Plays for Children no. 8), 1927, col. parcht wrappers by JMK, 38 + x pp., 6 in. × 5 in.

133 Percy Harman, *Reverie in B Minor* (pianoforte music), J. H. Laraway, London, 1927, (c) line drawing in blue and black by JMK, 13 in. × 10 in.

134 Louisa M. Alcott, *Little Women*, Collins (Collins' Bumper Reward Books no. 1), (1927), col. pict. paper bds by JMK, col. (fp) + col. (t) not by JMK, 7¾ in. × 5 in.

135 Louisa M. Alcott, *Little Wives*, Collins (Collins' Bumper Reward Books no. 2), (1927), col. pict. paper bds by JMK (*as 134*), col. (fp) + col. (t) not by JMK, 7¾ in. × 5 in.

136 Susan Coolidge, *What Katy Did at School*, Collins (Collins' Bumper Reward Books no. 3), (1927), col. pict. paper bds by JMK (*as 134*), col. (fp) + col. (t) not by JMK, 7¾ in. × 5 in.

137 Susan Coolidge, *What Katy Did*, Collins (Collins' Bumper Reward Books no. 4), (1927), col. pict. paper bds by JMK (*as 134*), col. (fp) + col. (t) not by JMK, 7¾ in. × 5 in.

138 Charles Lamb, *Tales From Shakespeare*, Collins (Collins' Bumper Reward Books no. 5), (1927), col. pict. paper bds by JMK (*as 134*), col. (fp) + col. (t) not by JMK, 7¾ in. × 5 in.

139 *Grimms Fairy Tales*, Collins (Collins' Bumper Reward Books no. 6), (1927), col. pict. paper bds by JMK (*as 134*), col. (fp) + col. (t) by J. R. Monsell, 256 pp., 7¾ in. × 5 in.

140 Lewis Carroll, *Alice in Wonderland*, Collins (Collins' Bumper Reward Books no. 7), (1927), col. pict. paper bds by JMK (*as 134*), col. (fp) + col. (t) + 30 b/w decs. by Winifred M. Ackroyd, 190 pp., 7¾ in. × 5 in.

141 *Andersen's Fairy Tales*, Collins (Collins' Bumper Reward Books no. 8), (1927), col. pict. paper bds by JMK (*as 134*), col. (fp) + col. (t) + b/w illus. by A. W. Bayes, 7¾ in. × 5 in.

142 *The Arabian Nights' Entertainments*, ed. Hon. Mrs Sugden, Collins (Collins' Bumper Reward Books no. 9), (1927), col. pict. paper bds by JMK (*as 134*), col. (fp) + col. (t) not by JMK, 7¾ in. × 5 in.

143 Charles Kingsley, *The Water Babies*, Collins (Collins' Bumper Reward Books no. 10), (?1928), col. pict. paper bds by JMK (*as 134*), col. (fp) + col. (t) not by JMK, 7¾ in. × 5 in.

144 F. W. Farrar, *Eric*, Collins (Collins' Bumper Reward Books no. 11), (?1928), col. pict. paper bds by JMK (*as 134*), col. (fp) + col. (t) not by JMK, 7¾ in. × 5 in.

145 Harriet Martineau, *Feats on the Fiord*, Collins (Collins' Bumper Reward Books no. 12), (?1928), col. pict. paper bds by JMK (*as 134*), col. (fp) + col. (t) not by JMK, 266 pp., 7¾ in. × 5 in.
In 1927 Jessie M. King also designed some of the covers, different from the one used for 'Collins' Bumper Reward Books', for a series entitled 'Collins' Bumper Rewards'. These were prize books for older children and were slightly

larger in format (8¼ in. × 5½ in.). They were priced at 2s 6d rather than the 2s of the 'Bumper Reward Books'. To confuse matters the new covers still carried the title 'Collins' Bumper Reward Books' but the titles were listed in the preliminaries as 'Popular Favourites'. The cover illustration of the 'Reward Books' was a knight in armour; that of the 'Rewards' was of children reading in a garden.

146 R. M. Ballantyne, *Coral Island*, Collins (Collins' Bumper Rewards no. 1), (1927), col. pict. paper bds by JMK, col. (fp) + col. (t) not by JMK, 8¼ in. × 5½ in.

147 R. M. Ballantyne, *The Gorilla Hunters*, Collins (Collins' Bumper Rewards no. 2), (1927), col. pict. paper bds by JMK (*as 146*), col. (fp) + col. (t) not by JMK, 8¼ in. × 5½ in.

148 R. M. Ballantyne, *Martin Rattler*, Collins (Collins' Bumper Rewards no. 3), (1927), col. pict. paper bds by JMK (*as 146*), col. (ep) + col. (t) not by JMK, 8¼ in. × 5½ in.

149 *Grimms Fairy Tales*, Collins (Collins' Bumper Rewards no. 4), (1927), col. pict. paper bds by JMK (*as 146*), col. (fp) + col. (t) not by JMK, 8¼ in. × 5½ in.

150 *Andersen's Fairy Tales*, Collins (Collins' Bumper Rewards no. 5), (1927), col. pict. paper bds by JMK (*as 146*), col. (fp) + col. (t) not by JMK, 8¼ in. × 5½ in.

151 Grace Marlow, *Book of Elves and Fairies*, Collins (Collins' Bumper Rewards no. 6), (1927), col. pict. paper bds by JMK (*as 146*), col. (fp) by J. R. Monsel, col. (t) by Ann Anderson, illus. by Charles Robinson and others, 286 pp., 8¼ in. × 5½ in.

152 R. M. Ballantyne, *The Young Fur Traders*, Collins (Collins' Bumper Rewards no. 7), (1927), col. pict. paper bds ? by JMK (*as 146*), col. (fp) + col. (t) not by JMK, 8¼ in. × 5½ in.

153 Mrs Henry Wood, *Danesbury House*, Collins (Collins' Bumper Rewards no. 8), (1927), col. pict. paper bds by JMK (*as 146*), col. (fp) + col. (t) not by JMK, 304 pp., 8¼ in. × 5½ in.

154 Nathaniel Hawthorne, *Tanglewood Tales*, Collins (Collins' Bumper Rewards no. 9), (1927), col. pict. paper bds by JMK (*as 146*), col. (fp) + col. (t) not by JMK, 8¼ in. × 5½ in.

155 R. M. Ballantyne, *The Red Eric*, Collins (Collins' Bumper Rewards no. 10), (1927), col. pict. paper bds ? by JMK (*as 146*), col. (fp) + col. (t) not by JMK, 8¼ in. × 5½ in.

156 John Drinkwater, *The Way of Poetry*, Collins (Collins' Dorian Booklets no. 1), (1927), pict. (ep) + pict. verso of (ht) + pict. (t) + decs. on each page by JMK, batik-style paper bds, green cloth spine, gilt, 5½ in. × 3½ in. Also brown leather, gilt with design in red, green, gold by JMK, boxed. Also (1928) suede-cloth, gilt.

157 *Omar Khayyám*, Collins (Collins' Dorian Booklets no. 2), (1927), (*as 156*). Also red leatherette gilt.

158 Eleanor Farjeon, *All The Year Round*, Collins (Collins' Dorian Booklets no. 3), (1927) (*as 156*).

159 Alice Meynel, *The School of Poetry*, Collins (Collins' Dorian Booklets no. 4), (1927) (*as 156*). Also with pictorial cover inscribed with the title.

160 *Flowers for Friendship*, Collins (Collins' Dorian Booklets no. 5), (1927) (*as 156*).

161 *Gems from Ella Wheeler Wilcox*, Collins (Colins' Dorian Booklets no. 6), (1927) (*as 156*), 92 pp. Also red leatherette gilt.

162 Arthur Cantillon, *Pierrot Before the Seven Doors*, trans. Hermon Ovid, Gowans & Gray (Repertory Plays no. 55), (1927), col. parcht wrappers by JMK, 38 pp., 6¼ in. × 4 in.

163 *Omar Khayyám*, Collins (Golden Dawn Booklets no. 1), (1928), pict. wrappers over card by JMK, sgd, pict. (ep) by JMK, pict. (t) by unnamed artist, 4 photogravure illus. after Charles Robinson, 32 unnumbered pp., 6 in. × 3 in. Supplied with envelope for mailing. Also plain gold wrappers with mtd label in yellow and green.

164 *Songs From Maurine*, (?), Collins (Golden Dawn Booklets no. 2), (1928) (*as 163*), but with line illus. by unnamed artist.

165 *Songs From Wilcox*, Collins (Golden Dawn Booklets no. 3), (1928) (*as 163*), but with line illus. by unnamed artist.

166 *Songs From Longfellow*, Collins (Golden Dawn Booklets no. 4), (1928) (*as 163*), but with pictorial title + 17 line illus. by J. A. Symonds.

167 *Songs From Byron*, Collins (Golden Dawn Booklets no. 5), (1928) (*as 163*), but with line illus. by H. E. Lock.

168 *Old English Songs*, Collins (Golden Dawn Booklets no. 6), (1928) (*as 163*), but with line illus. by J. A. Symonds.

169 *Youth and Love*, Collins (Golden Dawn

Booklets no. 7), (1928) (*as 163*), but with line illus. by A. Morrow.

170 *O Mistress Mine*, Collins (Golden Dawn Booklets no. 8), (1928) (*as 163*).

171 *Jacobite Lays*, Collins (Golden Dawn Booklets no. 9), (1928) (*as 163*), but with line illus. by J. A. Symonds.

172 *Little Queen*, Collins (Golden Dawn Booklets no. 10), (1928) (*as 163*), but with illus. by unnamed artist.

173 *A Phantom of Delights*, Collins (Golden Dawn Booklets no. 11), (1928) (*as 163*), but with illus. by unnamed artist.

174 William Blake, *Songs of Innocence*, Collins (Golden Dawn Booklets no. 12) (*as 163*), but with illus. by unnamed artist.

175 'Marion', *Mummy's Bedtime Story Book*, Cecil Palmer, 1929 (July), blue cloth with large col. pict. onlay by JMK, col. (fp) + col. (ep) + col. (t) + 11 full-page col. pl. + col. dec. on each page all by JMK, 56 pp., $11\frac{1}{2}$ in. × $8\frac{3}{4}$ in.

176 A. J. Talbot, *The Betrothal of the Princess*, Gowans & Gray (Repertory Plays no. 76), (1930), col. parcht wrappers by JMK, 20 + xii pp., $6\frac{1}{4}$ in. × 4 in.

177 Bessie Thomson Forrest, *Cinderella & Co*, Gowans & Gray, (1930), col. pict. paper bds by JMK, 56 pp., $8\frac{1}{2}$ in. × $6\frac{3}{4}$ in.

178 Henry C. Smith, *A Sprig of Rosemary*, Gowans & Gray (Repertory Plays no. 104), (1930), col. parcht wrappers by JMK, 37 pp., $6\frac{1}{4}$ in. × 4 in.

179 F. Sladon Smith, *The Resurrection of Joseph*, Gowans & Gray (Repertory Plays no. 95), (1931), col. parcht wrappers by JMK, 54 + x pp., 6 in. × 4 in.

180 Glen Hughes, *Cloaks*, Gowans & Gray (Repertory Plays no. 122), (1931), col. parcht wrappers by JMK, 25 pp., 6 in. × 4 in.

181 Katherine T. Rae, *The Gods Throw Incense*, Gowans & Gray (Repertory Plays no. 119), (1932), col. parcht wrappers by JMK, 22 pp., 6in. × 4in.

182 A. M. Williams, *A Bundle of Yarns*, Gowans & Gray, (1931), col. parcht wrappers by JMK, 88 + iv pp., 6 in. × 4 in.

183 George Burnett, *A Book of Scottish Verse*, Methuen, (1932), col. pict. d/w plus col. (fp) by JMK, blue cloth gilt, xvi + 208 + viii pp. Also 1937 orange cloth. Also 1937 blue cloth, smaller format.

184 *The Gallovidian Annual*, Robert Dinwiddie & Co, Dumfries (1932), 1 b/w illus. by JMK, 'Bran Sets Sail for the Isles', for M.C. Lochhead's *The Awakening*, stiff grey paper wrappers, $9\frac{1}{2}$ in. × $7\frac{1}{4}$ in.

185 *The Gallovidian Annual*, Robert Dinwiddie & Co, (1933), 1 b/w illus. by JMK, 'Everyone Knew', for *Ghaisties and Ferlies*, stiff grey paper wrappers, $9\frac{1}{2}$ in. × $7\frac{1}{4}$ in.

186 Jessie M. King, *Kirkcudbright: A Royal Burgh*, Gowans & Gray, 1934, col. parcht wrappers plus (t) plus 18 b/w illus. by JMK, 40 pp., $8\frac{3}{4}$ in. × $5\frac{1}{2}$ in.

187 Arthur Corder, *Our Lady's Garland*, De La More Press, London, 1934, pict. japon wrappers by JMK, pict. (t) plus dec. intro. page + 7 full-page and 9 other b/w illus. by JMK, 40 pp., $7\frac{3}{4}$ in. × $5\frac{1}{4}$ in.

188 *The Gallovidian Annual*, Robert Dinwiddie & Co, 1934, 1 b/w illus. by JMK, 'He made his herald blaw on his trumpet', for Lewis Spence's *Rashiecoat*, stiff grey paper wrappers, $9\frac{1}{2}$ in. × $7\frac{1}{4}$ in.

189 Florence Drummond, *The Fringes of Paradise*, Frederick Muller, 1935, col. pict. paper bds, by JMK, col. fp + 3 col. pl. by JMK, 48 pp., $7\frac{1}{2}$ in. × $4\frac{3}{4}$ in.

190 Kathleen Conygham Green, *The Two Bad Fairies*, Gowans & Gray (Plays for Children no. 11), 1935, col. parcht wrappers by JMK, 6 in. × 5 in.

191 *The Gallovidian Annual*, Robert Dinwiddie & Co, 1935, 1 b/w illus. by JMK, 'The Christ Child', for Margaret C. Lochhead's *Three Kings Rode West*, stiff grey paper wrappers, iv + 112 + ii pp., $9\frac{1}{2}$ in. × $7\frac{1}{2}$ in.

192 Margaret M. Guthrie, *War Waves*, pub. John Smith & Son, Glasgow (1942), d/w only with b/w halftone repro. of wash drawing by JMK, bds, 211 pp., $7\frac{1}{2}$ in. × 5 in.

193 Isobel K. C. Steele, *The Enchanted Capital of Scotland*, Plaid Publications, Edinburgh (1945), col. pict. d/w, b/w (fp), (t), 36 b/w, 4 double-page col. illus. all by JMK, blue cloth gilt, 54 pp., $9\frac{1}{2}$ in. × $7\frac{1}{2}$ in.

194 Revd James McCardel, *The Parish Church of New Kilpatrick*, Robert MacLehose & Co, Glasgow, 1949, col. d/w plus b/w (fp) of the same scene, by JMK, blue cloth gilt, 144 pp., $8\frac{3}{4}$ in. × $5\frac{1}{2}$ in. Also half-blue morocco.

Also, Bell & Bain Ltd, Glasgow, 1973, b/w
d/w only by JMK, blue cloth gilt.

C   *Books with reproductions of works by Jessie
     M. King not especially commissioned for the
     book and not reproduced elsewhere*

1   *The Studio*, vol. 14, 1898, 3 b/w illus. for Sir
    Edwin Arnold 'The Light of Asia'.

2   *The Studio*, vol. 15, 1899, 2 b/w illus. for
    'Wynken, Blynken and Nod'.

3   *The Studio*, vol. 17, 1899, 3 b/w book illus. for
    Wm. Morris 'The Wood at the World's End.'

4   *The Studio, Special Winter Number, 1899–1900,
    Modern Bookbindings & Their Designers*, 2
    b/w illus. of book covers.

5   *The Studio, Special Winter Number, 1900–2,
    Modern Pen Drawing*, 1 b/w illus. 'Pelleas and
    Melisande' (first version).

6   *The Studio*, vol. 24, 1902, 1 b/w illus. 'The
    Dance of the White Rose'.

7   *The Studio, Special Winter Number, 1902,
    Modern Designs in Jewellery and Fans*, 1 b/w
    illus. of a fan design.

8   *The Studio*, vol. 26, 1902, 11 b/w illus. in article
    'Miss Jessie M. King and her Work' by Walter
    R. Watson.

9   *Deutsche Kunst Und Dekoration*, vol. 10, 1902,
    b/w title-page + 5 b/w illus.

10 F. H. Newbery & George Fuchs, *'L'Exposition
    Internationale des Arts Décoratifs Modernes à
    Turin, 1902'*, 5 b/w illus.

11 *Arte Italiana 1902*, 2 b/w of book covers + 2
    b/w wrongly attributed to JMK.

12 Vittorio Pica, *L'Arte Decorativa All'
    Exposizione Di Torino 1902*, Bergamo, 1903, 2
    b/w illus. of book covers, 1 b/w illus. of
    drawing, 1 b/w illus. os screen, dec. grey paper
    wrappers.

13 *The Studio*, vol. 33, 1904, 2 b/w illus. of an
    embroidered curtain.

14 *The Studio*, vol. 33, 1904, 2 b/w illus. 'The Sea
    Shore' and 'Log Cabin'.

15 *The Art Journal*, 1905, b/w illus.

16 *Deutsche Kunst Und Dekoration*, vol. 15, 1905,
    4 b/w illus.

17 Walter Shaw Sparrow, *'Women Painters of the
    World'*, Hodder & Stoughton, 1905, 1 b/w illus.

'The Courtyard', beige cloth, green lettering not
by JMK, 332 pp., 12 in. × 8¼ in. Also suede, also
vellum, gilt.

18 *The Studio*, vol. 36, 1906, 6 b/w illus. of
    landscapes.

19 *The Studio Year Book of Decorative Art*, 1906,
    1 col. illus. of tile panel 'Ride a-Cock Horse', 1
    b/w illus. of wallpaper 'Sing a Song of
    Sixpence'.

20 *Deutsche Kunst Und Dékoration*, vol. 19, 1906,
    1 b/w photograph of JMK + 17 b/w illus.

21 *Art et Decoration*, 1907, 4 b/w illus.

22 *The Studio Year Book of Decorative Art*, 1907,
    1 b/w reproduction of fabric.

23 *The Art Journal*, 1907, 3 b/w illus.

24 *Art et Décoration*, 1908, 9 b/w illus.

25 *The Studio, Special Summer Number*, 1908,
    Colour Photography, 1 coloured (autochrome)
    photograph of JMK by J. Craig Annan.

26 *The Booklovers Magazine*, 1908, 9 b/w illus. in
    an article 'Miss Jessie M. King' by E. A. Taylor.

27 *The Studio Year Book of Decorative Art*, 1909,
    2 b/w reproductions of jewellery.

28 *The Odd Volume*, Simkin Marshall, 1909, 1
    b/w illus. 'The House of Fame', grey paper
    wrappers with mtd col. pl. by Monro Orr, xii +
    96 + lvi pp., 10½ in. × 7½ in.

29 *The Studio*, vol. 46, 3 b/w reproductions of
    bookplates.

30 *The Studio Year Book of Decorative Art*, 1910,
    1 col. reproduction of watercolour 'How Four
    Queens Found Sir Launcelot'.

31 *The Studio*, vol. 51, 1911, 1 col. reproduction of
    needlework panel 'How Four Queens Found Sir
    Launcelot'.

32 *The Studio Year Book of Decorative Art*, 1911,
    1 col. reproduction of needlework panel
    'Richard Yea and Nay'.

33 *The Studio, Special Winter Number, 1911–12,
    Pen, Pencil and Chalk*, 2 b/w illus. 'The Lament'
    and 'Peffer Mill House'.

34 *The Studio*, vol. 56, 1912, 1 col. reproduction of
    needlework panel 'Richard Coeur de Lion'.

35 *The Studio Year Book of Decorative Art*, 1912,
    1 col. illus. 'The Soul of Yvonne'.

36 *The Studio Year Book of Decorative Art*, 1913,
    1 col. illus. of fireplace design.

37 *The Odd Volume*, Simkin Marshall, 1913, 1 col. illus. 'A Reconsidered Proverb', blue/grey wrappers with mtd col. pl, xx + 96 + lx pp., 10½ in. × 7½ in.

38 P. Wylie Davidson, *Educational Metalcraft*, Longmans, Green & Co, 1913, 1 b/w reproduction of design by JMK for Glasgow School of Art badge, red cloth, 37 pp., 8½ in. × 6¾ in.

39 *Modern Book Illustrators and Their Work*, *The Studio*, 1914, 3 b/w illus., 'Aucassin and Nicolette', 'Youthe' and 'A Damsel of Passing Great Beauty', blue cloth gilt, viii + 192 pp., 11½ in. × 8¼ in.

40 *The Studio*, vol. 61, 1915, 3 b/w designs for *Ex Libris*.

41 *Paris Past and Present*, ed. E. A. Taylor, *The Studio*, 1915, 4 b/w illus. by JMK, printed grey wrappers, 200 pp., 11½ in. × 8 in.

42 *The Studio Year Book of Decorative Art*, 1915, 1 b/w illus. of design for an embroidered panel 'He Wanders in a Happy Dream'.

43 *The Thistle Souvenir Book*, John Horn Ltd, 1916, 1 b/w illus. 'The Princess Played with the Woodcutter's Daughter', 11 in. × 7¾ in.

44 *The Studio Year Book of Decorative Art*, 1917, 2 b/w reproductions of designs for printed cretonnes.

45 *The Studio*, vol. 60, 1913. Supplement 'Seven Happy Days' see B 109.

46 *The Studio Year Book of Decorative Art*, 1918, 1 col. reproduction of silk fabric 'The Gowan'.

47 *The Studio Year Book of Decorative Art*, 1922, 1 b/w illus. of batik panel 'The Queen Went a-Maying' (later reproduced in B 124).

48 *The Studio*, vol. 83, 1922, 1 b/w photograph of pottery by JMK.

49 *The Studio*, vol. 95, 1928, 1 col. reproduction + 1 b/w reproduction of landscapes.

50 Gerald and Celia Larner, *The Glasgow Style*, Paul Harris, 1970, 23 b/w photographs of works by JMK, black paper boards, 24 pp. + 147 unnumbered pp. of photographs, 9 in. × 8½ in. Also Astragal Books, 1980, pict. card covers.

51 *Jessie M. King and E. A. Taylor*, Paul Harris and Sotheby Belgravia, catalogue of the Glasgow Sale of 21 June 1977, numerous reproductions in b/w and colour, black paper boards, gilt, 94 pp., 8 in. × 8¼ in. Also stiff paper wrappers.

52 Julian Holsby, *Scottish Watercolours 1740–1940*, Batsford, 1980, 1 b/w illus. 'Good Fortune', blue cloth.

53 Victor Arwas, *Liberty Style*, Parco, Tokyo, 1983, 7 col. reproductions of jewellery/enamelwork by JMK, pict. card covers, 144 pp., 11½ in. × 8½ in.

54 Vivienne Becker, *Art Nouveau Jewellery*, Thames & Hudson, 1985, 4 b/w reproductions of jewellery by JMK, + one questioned item, 240 pp., dec. blue cloth, gilt.

55 Giovanni Fanelli and Enzio Godoli, *Art Nouveau Postcards*, Patrick Hawley, 1987, 1 col. reproduction of JMK postcard, 'The Queen of Hearts', 384 pp., 10¾ in. × 9 in.

56 Linda Parry, *Textiles of the Arts and Crafts Movement*, Thames & Hudson, 1988, 1 b/w illus. of JMK fabric 'Beauly', pict. card covers.

D *Books containing textual material by Jessie M. King other than in A, B or C.*
1. Gwen Cuthbert, *The Baby in the Glass*, A. Moring, (1930), col. fp + 3 illus. by Gwen Cuthbert, blue boards with pict. onlay, 23 pp., 9 in. × 6½ in., preface by JMK.

E *Exhibition catalogues, posters, programmes and advertisement ephemera commissioned from Jessie M. King.*
1 The Classical English Drama (F. R. Benson's Company), The Royalty Theatre, Glasgow, 1900. Cover for prospectus.

2 The Glasgow Society of Artists, 1903. Exhibition catalogue.

3 Glasgow School of Art Students Annual Dance, 1903. Invitation.

4 Miss Cranston's Tea Rooms, Glasgow, 1903. Advertisement folder.

5 Bruton Street Galleries, London, 1905. Poster, season ticket and catalogue for exhibition of work by JMK.

6 Gowans & Gray, c 1905. Printed postcard.

7 Variety performance in aid of the San Francisco Disaster Fund, Glasgow, 1906. Programme cover.

8 Miss Cranston's Tea Rooms, Glasgow, 1906. Menu card.

9 T & R Annan and Sons, Glasgow, 1907. Handbill, invitation card and catalogue for exhibition of work by JMK.

Index